Diana Baleanu was born in Bucharest, Romania, in the 1970s. As the daughter of a diplomat, she spent her early years living between Bucharest and her father's diplomatic posts. Following her father's defection to the West in 1987, Diana and the rest of the family were forced to remain in Romania and face persecution from the tyrannical communist government of the time.

Reunited with her father after the collapse of the Iron Curtain, she now lives in England with her two daughters and husband and enjoys a career in teaching.

To the great women in my life who have taught me and continue to teach me how to stand strong and persevere – no matter what path life might take.

And for Dad, who had the courage to stand up to injustice and do the right thing.

***

"Should you ever find yourself the victim of other people's bitterness, ignorance, smallness or insecurities, remember, things could be worse…

You could be them."

Proverb

Diana Baleanu

AGAINST THE ODDS

To Beth,
Remember to always follow your heart & enjoy your life's magic!
Diana x

AUSTIN MACAULEY PUBLISHERS™
LONDON · CAMBRIDGE · NEW YORK · SHARJAH

Copyright © Diana Baleanu (2018)

The right of Diana Baleanu to be identified as author of this work has been asserted by her in accordance with section 77 and 78 of the Copyright, Designs and Patents Act 1988.

All rights reserved. No part of this publication may be reproduced, stored in a retrieval system, or transmitted in any form or by any means, electronic, mechanical, photocopying, recording, or otherwise, without the prior permission of the publishers.

Any person who commits any unauthorised act in relation to this publication may be liable to criminal prosecution and civil claims for damages.

Some names and identifying details have been changed to protect the privacy of individuals.

A CIP catalogue record for this title is available from the British Library.

ISBN 9781528909822 (Paperback)
ISBN 9781528909839 (E-Book)

www.austinmacauley.com

First Published (2018)
Austin Macauley Publishers Ltd™
25 Canada Square
Canary Wharf
London
E14 5LQ

With my deepest gratitude to the team at AM Publishers for taking a chance on an unknown writer and making a dream come true.

Where shall I start the story of my life? Before I was even born, in the 1940s? Or maybe in my teens, in the 1980s? Though perhaps my story is starting just now, spending time with friends, chatting without inhibitions, enjoying having all of my family around me, looking at them with a carefree smile on my face, teaching at a secondary school and, in doing so, making the most of my life.

Mmm…my life was not always as smooth as it might look now from the outside. The path which I have travelled to get here, to this very ordinary life, was, for some time, as treacherous as it was extraordinary. But if I was to do it all over again, I doubt if I'd change a thing. Let me know what you think!

I was born in communist Romania at the beginning of the 1970s, a Communist bloc country under the rule of a totalitarian, one-party regime which as time went on, was becoming increasingly capricious, abusive and brutal. At the head of it, was its absolute leader, Nicolae Ceausescu. To his opponents, Ceausescu was an unpredictable despot, instilling in his people a terrifying fear through the brutality of his secret service, the *Securitate*, whilst doing his utmost to accumulate a huge, personal wealth derived mainly from the sale of the country's natural resources and mineral riches. And while he was shamelessly flaunting his wealth, most Romanians lived in deprivation, with lack at every level of their existence. Their daily lives revolving around mere survival, as increasingly worsening austerity measures were starting to be put in place.

Lack of free press. Given how all aspects of the media were under the control of the state, meant that the distribution of any kind of information which was not state approved, was consequently banned. Anyone caught in the process of taking part in any such activity, risked severe punishment, would be arrested, interrogated, physically and psychologically abused and degraded, sentenced and imprisoned.

Lack of energy, resulted in frequent power cuts and endless evenings spent in dimness, as households would huddle around a few lit candles. Evenings in the winter months were especially difficult given how besides the lack of electricity, people were also left wondering if tonight might be the night when the heating would kick in or the hot water might start to run for long enough to be able to have a coveted hot shower or bath.

Though, above it all, the lack of food was the lack that reigned supreme. And with it, the never ending queues at market stalls, outside food stores and bakeries, alongside a flourishing black market in foodstuffs, which was becoming the norm.

On the other hand, what Romania did not lack, was an abundance of spies; agents working for Ceausescu's dreaded secret services, the *Securitate*. And they were everywhere! Every community, every place of work, every block of flats was believed to have at least one agent reporting back to the regime every detail and every aspect of people's lives – from the everyday, insignificant matters, to any perceived criticism of the regime, to possible plots against Ceausescu. And in doing so, they would be feeding amongst ordinary people the feeling of debilitating fear, of terror. A fear of the brutal consequences and repercussions of being caught doing something that you should not be doing.

And so, such was the landscape of the country, around the time that I was born.

As for my parents, my mother, Gina, was a free-spirited, opinionated, strikingly beautiful, fashion-loving, incredibly funny yet super smart dentist; and my father, Virgil, was a serious, quiet, book-loving, hardworking diplomat. I was their first child and I came along shortly after they had completed their University studies, just as they were embarking on their respective careers.

My mother, Gina, came from a family of German ancestry; her grandparents, having found themselves for business and commercial reasons, living in Transylvania at the turn of the previous century, a part of the world which back then belonged to the Austrian-Hungarian Empire. But, given a twist of fate, at the end of the First World War, Transylvania became part of Romania. And whilst my great-grandparents continued to live there in harmony for more than 20 years after this event, once the communists came to power, following the Second World War, everything changed. Just like that, my great-grandparents found themselves destitute, literally overnight, at the hands of the new rulers, the newly formed and Stalin-backed Romanian communist regime.

The story goes that they came to my great-grandparents' home as they always did – in the middle of the night whilst the family was fast asleep and unsuspecting inside the house, to be awoken to a living nightmare. They burst in, they forced their way inside their house, they rammed their guns in their terrified faces and they hauled them out of their beds. They were told how all of their property was to be seized, '*nationalised*'. Their home, their factories, their possessions, all of their personal belongings gone in a bewildered blink of an eye. All of their possessions, that was, bar a few items of jewellery which my great-grandmother managed to smuggle in her nightgown's pockets in the belief that should it ever come to it, they might be able to rely on the sale of the jewels as leverage for survival.

However, my great-grandparents did not only have their possessions taken away, but their identities too, with new ones being thrust upon them whilst having their previous ones completely erased. Just as their birth certificates and identity documents were thrown on the bonfire, new ID documents, bearing their new Romanian names and citizenship, were handed to them. My great-grandparents, alongside so many others who faced the same fate, did not have the luxury of protesting against it or of even expressing an opinion on the matter, as all this had been done under the watchful eye of armed soldiers...

By the time I was born, even though some 30-odd years had passed since those events, my great-grandmother's, and subsequently my grandparents' and my mother's resentfulness and disdain towards communism, and particularly the communists they were living alongside of, was still raging just as potently.

My father, Virgil, on the other hand, came from a family which had long-standing ties with communism. In fact, you could say his grandparents were the godparents of communism. His grandfather had been a communist party activist who fought throughout the Second World War to overthrow the fascist government of Romania whilst putting together a shadow communist party ready to take over the leadership of the country in the instance of when fascism was to be overthrown and defeated. I hope you're paying close attention, for events similar to these will prove to be the underlining themes of my life too. Just like history itself, they will come to repeat themselves in my immediate family and within my lifetime, too.

Where was I? Oh, my paternal great-grandfather. A Marxist through and through, who would find himself in and out of prison for organising unions and workers to strike as a mark of dissent against the existing government of the 1930s and '40s. Tried several times in different military courts, he would frequently end up in prison, quite often alongside his closest ally, the man who would come to lead the post-war Romania and who would become the first general secretary of the country.

And it was during one of these prison spells that they came across a young man, a boy really, for he was probably no older than 17 or so, by the name of Nicu, who had been finding himself in the same prison, mainly due to repeated petty theft and street fighting. But what an opportunity for the activists, who would be kept apart from most of the other convicts, for they befriended this young Nicu and persuaded him to contact their comrades on the outside with instructions on how to move the fight onwards, to drive the cause forward. Of course, in return, Nicu, who came from a dirt poor family, was to enjoy the hospitality of my great-grandmother, also an activist. My great-grandfather assured him that she would offer him bed (albeit in the loft of the house) and board in their spacious house, just outside Targoviste. For Nicu, the offer of free shelter and food was more than a good deal.

Besides hospitality, my great-grandmother also offered Nicu guidance related to making contact with the activists on the outside and spreading the word of those inside the prison. And in doing so, Nicu found himself gradually taking part, more and more, in spreading manifestos and enabling gatherings where communist strategies would be discussed. Nicu took to his new duties like a duck to water! He was such a good, reliable boy, full of initiative, too! Yes, Nicu grew up in and out of prison, regularly getting himself caught stealing and brawling, in order to get close enough to my great-grandfather and his partner in arms so that he can pass information to and from the activists on the outside. Oh, yes, Nicu grew up as such and before long, he grew in stature, too, for you might recognise him by his full name, Nicolae Ceausescu, who, in 1965, became the second Secretary General of Romania and was later so infamously executed on TV by a firing squad in 1989, following Romania's bloody revolution.

Ceausescu continued to follow my great-grandmother's guidance, well beyond her husband's death in the late '40s. And when her guidance was no longer as sharp as it used to be, due to old age, well…there was her son to take over where she left off. My grandfather, my father's father, became one of Ceausescu's most trusted inner-circle advisors, hunting buddy, tennis partner and, together with their respective wives, regular dinner companions.

So it was quite obvious to me, even from a very young age, that I had been born into a family of painful dichotomy. On one hand, there was my mother and her side of the family, holding on to their values, traditions, language, beliefs and principles, including respect to personal freedoms and belief in the Christian faith.

On the other hand, there was my father and his side of the family, where personal freedoms were expected and required to be surrendered in favour of the greater good ("How many of these freedoms are Ceausescu and your father surrendering? I really do want to know," my maternal great-grandmother would shout at my father when she'd become annoyed by some comment that he would make), religion had no place, for the head of state enjoyed God-like status and ethnic minorities within the country were treated with suspiciousness at the very best, as if they were the enemy.

There were regular fights between my parents as well. They all centred on life values and beliefs, including how I should or shouldn't be brought up. My first spoken language ended up being German, given how I was looked after mainly by my mother and maternal grandmother. This was something by which my father was beyond embarrassed in the company of his own family and I remember always getting the talk before a visit from them, about making sure that I ought to speak only in Romanian, not a word in German!

Once, when I was about the age of five or six, I innocently asked my paternal grandparents if they were to visit us on Christmas Day, my father turned beetroot red and looked furiously in both my direction and my mother's. My mother, in return, started laughing in delight, head thrown back, then catching my father's eye, defiantly saying, "Why would the whole country have Christmas Day off if not for celebrating it?"

My paternal grandfather tried to put the record straight immediately by saying, "It's for a general holiday purpose so that the workers of our country can enjoy a well-deserved rest, it's not for the purpose of any particular celebrations."

Though years later, I wondered if that casual, though defiant, remark of my mother's might have given my paternal grandfather certain thoughts about holidays and their purpose. As from future years, working people were no longer afforded Christmas Day off, just a couple of days off around New Years' Eve – obviously, not a religious festival, so OK to celebrate.

My paternal grandfather, in his fatherly pride, saw my father as his greatest tool in furthering his own Marxist beliefs by building ties with those of similar ideology abroad or by trying to undermine those of different ideology, also abroad. Thus, my father, under his father's guidance and at his insistence, was thrust into a career in the diplomatic service. His fluency in French and English at a time when few in the country spoke foreign languages made him a perfect candidate for service, firstly in North Africa and the Middle East and then, a longer period of service in London. And whilst in London, fulfilling to begin with, his duty as Second Secretary to the Ambassador, he was to serve, at the same time, and at his father's bequest, as an undercover Secret Service Operative which, technically for you and me, translates as an undercover spy.

So, I guess you could say that for a while, I had quite the privileged life by any standards, never mind the standards of communist Romania of the '70s and '80s. Whilst in London, we lived in an apartment within the vast Ambassadorial Residence in Belgravia. I went to an exclusive primary school, my school friends having similar privileged backgrounds of diplomatic service, or old money or even new money... We all lived pretty much within the square mile of Belgravia and Knightsbridge and knew little of life beyond it. Besides school, my life revolved around tennis, ballet, playing the violin, swimming and drinking hot chocolate with my friends on Saturday mornings in the Harvey Nichols top floor café whilst our mothers shopped downstairs for glamorous dresses to wear at that evening's social event hosted by some head of state or monarch or such other. Truth be told, besides the occasional visits to Harvey Nichols or Peter Jones, I saw little of my mother during this time, as she was always busy preparing or getting ready for evening receptions or dinners, sometimes at our residence, sometimes elsewhere. I saw my father even less, as he usually worked without fail six days a week, leaving earlier than I would wake up in the mornings and not returning until way past my bedtime. I was, however, incredibly close to my sister, my lovely, smiley, baby sister, who, at eight years younger than me, was the centre of my world.

A few years after having moved there, London had become almost everything I could remember, having only had returned to Romania briefly, for one summer vacation, the previous year.

And then, one day, out of the blue, I remember my father turning up at my school unexpectedly. It was just before lunchtime, so not quite time to go home yet. Besides, I couldn't even ever recall my father coming to pick me up from school. Yet, there he was, talking to my teacher in hushed voices, having entered my classroom with the head teacher in tow. After a few more exchanges, all three of them came up to me and explained that I had to say goodbye to my classmates and friends for now, as I was supposed to return, as a matter of urgency, back to Romania, together with my family. Confused and bewildered, given I had not anticipated this to happen, I said my goodbyes, uncertain of what was going on…

We finally leave the school behind us, get into our car and on our way back to the residence, my father starts explaining that my grandfather, his father, had passed away that morning and that we had to return to Romania for his funeral. We arrive back at our residence in Belgravia, where, up in the apartment, we are met by the image of my mother sat on the sofa in the living room, watching TV, face like thunder, trying her best to ignore our arrival.

My father starts to hover around, looking at me, as if considering carefully what to say next. In the end, he settles for, "Gina, you need to start packing." It sounds as if he is almost pleading with her.

My mother, in return, studiously ignores him and continues to pretend that she is engrossed in her TV programme, though I can tell by the expression on her face that she is not quite following whatever it may be…

"Fine, I'll start then. I'll start with the girls' clothes…" snaps my father, opening and closing wardrobe doors, looking completely lost as to where to start.

A few seconds pass and then my mum finally turns around to face my father.

"You can't go back there! We can't go back! You risk being put in front of a firing squad! With your father dead, you are a dead man now, too! They will kill you! And then what will happen to us? To me and the kids?" she says, both aggressively and pleadingly at the same time.

The outburst takes me by surprise, and truth be told is making me feel a little scared. I understand what she is saying and I understand the gravity of the situation, though none of it is making any sense to me. *Dead man? They will kill you?* Those words were clear enough but so shocking to hear them being addressed to my father. *Why would my mother be using them at my father's address?* That, I could categorically not understand. My heart pounding, I feel terrified, feel like crying, feel like screaming at my mum at the top of my lungs, "What is going on? What are you talking about?" But, at the same time, I feel like it is not really my place to question anything, and so no tears leave my eyes and no words come out. I keep it all inside.

"Please, Gina, let's not go through all this again…" I hear my father pleading with a hopeless sigh. "It will be fine. Nobody suspects a thing. Besides, we have to go back. It's my father's funeral in three days' time. I can't not go. I have to pay my respects."

"OK," my mother answers back. "Say that no one suspects anything yet. We go back, bury your father. And then what? We come back here and carry on until eventually they do find out for certain? It will still come to the same result!"

After a moment of thought my father replies, trying to pacify her, "We will come back. We will put together a plan. It will work out. We'll be OK. I promise. I won't let any harm come to the family."

I don't know what persuaded my mother, but eventually and reluctantly she relents. We pack, we get into a car, go to the airport, board the plane and return to Romania for my grandfather's funeral. Only a short visit before returning to my life in London, back to my school and to my friends. Or so I thought…

Stepping off the plane after a four-year absence, everything in Romania seems alien. They say that children are great at picking up new things, but they are also great at forgetting. And I had pretty much completely forgotten the life I had lived there beforehand, forgotten the land and the family I had left behind. I'm 12 years old, and getting off the plane I am shocked to be welcomed by such an austere, bleak urban landscape, an oppressive heat and masses of people walking everywhere or waiting at bus stops with distinct sadness written all over their faces. Yes, my mother had warned me that the landscape would be shockingly depressing but nothing has prepared me for this, above all the miserable, desolate, at times desperate look in people's eyes.

"Why isn't anyone smiling? Why does everyone look so sad?" I ask as the car drives through the streets of Bucharest on our way to our home.

I am met at first by deadly silence. But eventually my mother replies, "Life. Lack. Lack of food. Lack of money. Uncertainty. Survival, for most people here, is an everyday battle. People always having to queue up for hours on end for the little food which is made available to them. Tough, sometimes inhumane, working conditions. Unreliable, overcrowded, often dangerous public transport. Cars are too expensive for many to afford. And the living conditions are not any better either. Hot water, heating and even electricity sometimes cut off for days on end…" my mother tries to explain.

I think about the prospect of having a cold shower on a hot day such as this and that doesn't seem so unbearable, quite on the contrary. But, then I consider having the same cold shower in the middle of a freezing cold, snowy winter when temperatures would easily plummet below 10 degrees Centigrade, and I shudder at the thought.

"Above all else, there is no hope," my mother carries on. "No hope for a better life. Or even a different life. No hope, beyond living day to day, for mere survival."

The car falls silent as we all consider in our private ways the words we just heard spoken. A few seconds later, I hear my father, so softly whispering I almost think I imagine it. "Change will come. Whatever may be, I'll make sure of it…"

Hearing this, at first, my mother turns her head away, to stare blankly out of the window at the passing landscape, before quietly saying as if to herself, "Mmm… Will it?"

I can't remember much of what followed those few weeks – my grandfather's funeral no doubt, though I wasn't allowed to go due to my age (open casket, there would have been no way my mother would have allowed it for me to be there) so I can't exactly remember much about that event. Perhaps a family weekend at the seaside and visiting family, my beloved maternal grandparents and my much adored great-grandmother whom I hadn't even realised how much I had missed and whom it was so wonderful to see again after such a long absence.

Time is nearing towards the end of the summer, and also towards the end of our time in Romania. My mum and I are just starting to talk about things we would have to do once back in London, like buying a new uniform for the new school year and getting back to the daily routine, when my father, who had been at work at his office in Bucharest for the past few weeks, comes home one lunchtime, looking crestfallen. He walks into the kitchen where my mum and I are, and slumps down on a chair at the kitchen table, putting his head in his hands. My mum watches him with a frown but carries on setting the dinner table without asking him anything. After a few silent moments, my father starts talking, almost in a whisper, his voice cracking with emotion, "Diana is no longer allowed to join us in London…"

"What?" my mother screeches back immediately, violently jumping up from her chair and throwing the knife she was using to one side. And for a split second, as she leaps towards my father, I think she might just hit him. Instead, I watch as if in slow motion, as she furiously walks up and stands over him, hand on hips.

"What did you just say?" she shouts at him, her voice quivering with the sound of desperation, whilst I, myself, feeling suddenly anxious to the point of being nauseous, try to digest the meaning of the words uttered by my father.

"I've been told today, this morning... I have been given back our passports in preparation for our return to London next week, but Diana's was not among them. When I asked for hers, I was told that when we will return next week, we will have to do so without her..."

Straight away, without missing a beat, my mum, still looking furiously at my father, says, "They know. The God damned bastards know! They must do! But they don't have proof. So they're keeping our daughter hostage in return. Well, tell them we're not going without her!"

"I did," my father replies, dejected. "You think that was not the first thing I said to them? But, they said that's not an option. And given that circumstance, I'd be relieved of all my duties and responsibilities in my current role," he finishes by saying.

"Relieved of your duties? You should have listened to me back in London!" hisses my mum, now full of anger and disdain at my father's address. "We should not have come back here! You should have defected, like I asked you to! You said to me back there that everything will be fine! This is the furthest point from fine as I can imagine! How could you do this to us, to your family?"

And on and on the conversation goes as I look bewildered from one of my parents to another, trying to follow what is being said, as if watching a game of tennis. It's a conversation I played and replayed in my mind over and over again over time. I was heartbroken. Not just because I couldn't go back to London, couldn't resume the routine I was used to, in a place that had become home to me. But mostly, because this meant, above all else, that I couldn't see and be with my darling, little sister every day anymore. And that was worse than a dagger to my young heart.

For the remainder of the week, I put on a brave face, being cheerful to all around me even though deep inside my heart was bleeding. When the time comes, I even manage to smile and reassure my parents as I say goodbye to them all, even though my eyes are stinging from wanting to cry and my throat feels so tight I can't swallow, for I fear that if I would start crying, I would never be able to stop.

Family separation, one of the most heinous things to happen to a human being, and routinely used by tyrannical governments around the world as a weapon against those they want to persecute. Now, at an older age, I have come accept it, on a good day I might even be able to rationalise it. Though back then, as a child and even later as a teen and young adult, I found it difficult to accept and come to terms with, and blamed the 'damned communists' my grandparents continued to rage about with renewed pathos, but also both my parents, for the sense of loss I was left with following their return to London, particularly because I was so close and so fond of my little sister.

Still, somehow, following their departure, I managed to adapt to my new life with my maternal grandparents and great-grandmother, but a feeling of sadness and melancholy would follow me everywhere. My parents and little sister would never be far from my thoughts, and family occasions such as birthdays and Christmases would no longer be an opportunity for joy and celebration, but one of sadness due to the painful absence of loved ones and an ever present sense of loneliness. Despite my grandparents' best efforts and intentions to keep me constantly busy and entertained as well as showered in their affection, I would be acutely missing the family which was now so far away and with which I had so little contact. Back in communist Romania, in the days before mobile phones, FaceTime and Skype, you could not just merely pick up the phone and make a call abroad, for international calls were banned. And my parents were only allowed to make one call a month back to Romania, though sometimes my mum would break that rule and call a bit more often. On one hand, I would so look forward to and would actually live for those phone calls, though on the other hand, hearing my little sister's voice would make me want to be next to her and hug her so badly. The phone calls would only make me feel worse rather than better, serving only to intensify the physical gulf between us...

One year passes and my parents are supposed to come back to Romania to visit me for the summer. It's only a few days before their expected arrival. It is a warm summer's day and I am out at the park, playing with my friends, when one of them comes up to me saying, "Diana, Your parents have just arrived home!"

"What?" I say, surprised by the news and unsure whether to believe her or not. "They're not supposed to arrive until the weekend. It's only Wednesday."

"No, they're definitely here," she retorts. "I saw them getting out of the taxi myself. They're at the house."

My heart pounding with excitement and anticipation, I start running towards our house, faster and faster, until I see that I'm getting closer and closer to the glass front door. But, given how fast I'm running, I know that I can't slow myself down enough to avoid a collision with the door. So, I put my hands out in front, hoping that the door is not locked and that I can push it open. As I do so, the glass panel of the door smashes around me and I realise that I had just dived through the shattered panel of the door. I'm on the floor and conscious but I feel a hot sensation on my face. Straight away, I hear a door opening upstairs and my mum's voice saying, "Diana? Is that you?"

"Yes, Mum it's me. Welcome home!" I try to sound chirpy whilst looking behind me at the now destroyed door and thinking how I'd explain the damage to it. I slowly try to get up, dabbing at the wetness on my face, wondering where it might have come from. My mum comes down the stairs, looks at me and gasps in shock.

"Oh, my good God!" she says, "You're covered in blood! Where is the wound?" she wants to know and starts closely inspecting my face.

Well, as it turns out, in having flown through the glass door, I had also cut my nose, not off, luckily, but enough to cause a gushing wound. My mum helps me up, walks me upstairs, sits me down and starts cleaning and patching me up.

Finally, she says, "Well, that's one way of making an entrance! The wound is more superficial than anything, but you will be left with a scar right here, on the bridge of your nose…"

But I don't care, all I really care about at that moment is seeing my little sister. I had missed her so much, every day for the past year, all I want to do is squeeze her in my arms at long last. Just then, my little sister walks into the living room, and I can tell she'd been asleep as she's still rubbing the sleep dust off her eyes. We see each other across the room, and immediately run to each other and kiss and hug each other tight. I thought that after this absence of one year, she would no longer recognise me or that she might feel awkward around me, but luckily that's not the case. She's just as happy to see me. *Life can't get much better than this!* I think to myself.

Before having returned back home for this summer holiday, my understanding was that my parents were to spend only a few weeks in Romania before resuming their posting in London. I realised long before those weeks were up that they were not, in fact, going to return to London and that they had come back for good.

During the daytime there was a frosty politeness between my parents and a peculiar, constant, jumpy nervousness about my mother. At night, however, my world would turn into an inescapable nightmare as I could hear my parents' constant, furious and bitter arguing, possibly in the belief that both my sister and I would be sound asleep and so unable to overhear them. But I'd hear them alright. My mother would shout angrily at my father over and again.

"This stupidity of yours will get us both killed! We shouldn't have come back! Even without Diana there, we shouldn't have come back here! They would have eventually allowed her to join us over there! In actual fact, we shouldn't have come back here when your father died, when Diana was still there with us!"

Whilst my father would reply equally angry, "And what about them? These people? They deserve better! They deserve a better life, a better future! The situation in this country can't go on as it is! The situation is helpless and hopeless! It's got to be changed! You can see for yourself how desperate things have become – the lack of food, the lack of jobs, the lack of proper education, the lack of human respect and decency! Someone needs to make a stand for them, we need to make a change!"

At which my mum would retort, "You can't serve the people of this country from behind bars. You won't be able to make a change if you're put in front of a firing squad. You would have had a better chance of bringing about change from the outside of the country, of the system. From here, from inside this country, you will never be able to change anything! You, one man, are not enough to fight the system. And meanwhile, you are foolishly risking not just your life, but your whole family's life, too!"

And so it would go on and on every night, backwards and forward, with some nights my mum being angry and aggressive at my dad, some other nights tearful and pleading, and sometimes impassive or sarcastic. Nothing was discussed with me, or in front of me, but by then I was becoming old enough to figure out from their nightly rows that my father was somehow planning to change the current political system, to a more decent way of life for the many. However, my mother feared that, given the political regime of Romania at the time, and its notoriety to brutally suppress and dispose of any form of criticism or dissent, could only mean one thing: That my father's plans would have dramatic, nefarious consequences for him and obviously us too, his family.

Even though the nightly rows unsettled me and the implications of what was being said would make me fret in the moment, by daytime I wouldn't really give much thought to it anymore. By then I was 13 years old, and enjoyed the things that 13-year-olds around the world probably enjoy. The company of friends, listening to music together, avidly reading the pop magazines that my dad would bring home from work and also being passionate about fashion and really good at making clothes, a skill I had started to teach myself the previous year and which I enjoyed more and more thanks to all the Vogue, Tatler and Prima fashion magazines my mum had brought back from London. The days would come and go, life would fall into some kind of routine and after a while even the frost between my parents seemed to melt somewhat.

Summer is long gone when one day, my father comes home from work, late, as ever. It's almost dinner time, so we all sit down at the kitchen table for an evening meal. My mother talks about her day at work – being a dental surgeon, she returned back to work shortly after the end of the summer – and by way of making conversation she asks my father about his day, too. He casually answers, "I've been asked to go on a week-long delegation to Vienna, next month, in November." My mother asks if the family would be allowed to go with him, to which he says, "No, just myself and one other guy." I don't give much importance to this conversation and the following weeks carry on as expected, my days being taken with school, friends and the ordinary things I guess all 13–14-year-olds around the world must do.

The time eventually arrives for my father to start preparing for the trip. The evening before his departure, with the suitcase packed, flight tickets and passport at the ready and firmly placed on top of the suitcase, my father finds himself home in time to go out for a family meal. So, all four of us go out to a restaurant, to one of those hotels just outside the centre of Bucharest, which my mum was fond of, not so much due to the food, but more so due to the greenery and pretty gardens surrounding them. So, we have a family meal out that night, the night before his departure to Vienna and when we get back home, before going to bed, he says his goodbyes to my sister and me. Nothing out of the ordinary you might think, but to me, for some reason, it feels peculiar, as he insists on hugging me for a long while, which I can't remember him ever having done before. Not the over affectionate my father; nor myself for that matter. And then he carries on, saying, "You'll have to look after Anna for me really well. And your mum, too. Until we see each other again, whenever that might be." I look at him a little puzzled by his words, and I swear he has tears in his eyes. I feel uncomfortable by all this sudden, out of place display of affection which I'm not used to from my father and try to brush it off.

"Well, we'll see each other in a week's time, won't we? That's not that long, after all we've been apart for longer…" I answer, sounding as if I am trying to reassure him or maybe myself.

But then he looks at me with a sad look on his face, swallows hard and replies, "We'll see each other again, that's for sure." Which leaves me going to bed that night slightly anxious and thinking, *What a weird thing to say! I hope he's not seriously ill and going abroad for treatment or something…*

My father leaves early the following morning, too early for me to see him off so when I wake up, I get myself and my little sister, Anna, ready and we make our way to school. When I get back from school, my mother is at home, which surprises me as even though she was supposed to go to the airport with my father, thereafter she was going straight to work and so she was not expected home until later on in the afternoon. But, here she is at home, and she's quietly and furiously pacing the living room, the hallway and her bedroom, throwing things from an open wardrobe into a small burgundy hold-all bag. Eventually, she says to me, "You need to take this bag to one of your friends' houses. Ask them to look after it for us for a while."

"Why?" I dare ask.

"Stop asking questions, I don't need to answer to you! Just do as you're told!" she says defensively. I'm shocked at her abruptness and my face probably betrays my feelings for she stops what she's doing, sits herself down on the sofa next to me, and looks me in the eyes.

"Jewellery – Mutti and Mammy's stuff. And a bit of cash. We need to keep it safe somewhere. Things will turn very ugly, very quickly for a while, I'm certain of it. I have a feeling our survival might depend on what's in this bag," she says softly. "And I don't think our house will be safe for much longer, either," she adds before zipping up the bag and placing it on my lap. I look at the bag and then I look at my mum, confused and puzzled.

"What are you talking about?" I ask her nervously, suddenly filled with panic and fear. As a child, as a human being even, you are made to believe that your house, your home, is the most sacred, the safest place on earth. What had possibly gotten into my mother? What was she talking about? And why was she acting so crazy? She was starting to scare me and my little sister was picking up on the vibes, and crying the place down. I quickly try to think which one of my friends wouldn't question too much such a request and would accept to look after the bag, in order to calm my mother down, but also just to get out of the house as the atmosphere is stifling me. In the end, I decide on a neighbour friend, so my mother tells me that I need to go by myself, without my little sister, and to go straight away.

"And don't tell her that I put you up to it! Just make it look as if it's some of your rubbish she's looking after for a while..." As I am about to leave, I catch a glimpse of one of my mum's Vogue magazines lying around on the dining room table, and I quickly grab it on my way out. Me and my friend we can take a look at some of the dresses in the magazine and maybe start planning a few ideas, a few outfits, I figure, for the New Year's Eve party which we were invited to, at another mutual friend's house. *Then, at the weekend maybe we could go into town together,* I think, *and buy some fabric so then I can start making our outfits. Can't wait!*

I get to my friend's house, she welcomes me inside and then we go to her bedroom, where I ask her to stash the bag for me. "Christmas presents for my family, I don't want them, especially my little sister, to see them." I tell her and she winks, takes it without asking any questions and kicks it under her bed. We chat for a while, listen to some music, leaf through the Vogue magazine, talk about some outfit ideas, and then I figure it's time for me to get back home. I leave the Vogue magazine with my friend as her mum had caught a glimpse of it, and she wants to have a look, as well. "Diana, you always spoil us so with all these wonderful magazines. And your sewing and dress making is out of this world! We'll be putting our orders in for Christmas soon!" she says and I tell her she's being too kind about my dress making skills, but at the same time I feel incredibly proud. Then, I say my goodbyes and go back home, a feeling of dread overwhelming me at the prospect of seeing my mum in the state in which I had left her earlier.

I walk into the house, and it becomes obvious straight away that my mother is still in a heightened emotional state, now smoking furiously, which she hadn't done in years, and still pacing up and down the house. Since she doesn't seem inclined to be preparing any dinner and I don't want to incur an outburst from her, I go into the kitchen and start to make something to eat for me, my mum and sister. In the end though, it's only my sister and I eating as my mum is not interested, and afterwards we go to bed. The following morning, my sister and I go to school as per our usual routine, and my mum goes to work. My mum seems to have calmed down since the previous evening, but she is far from chirpy and the dark circles under her eyes and haunted expression betray a rough, sleepless night.

I am happy to be at school, surrounded by my friends and try my hardest to get involved in lessons in the classroom and conversations at playtime, in order to forget the events of home and of the previous evening. The last lesson of the day, maths, just starts when I see a woman whom I recognise to be the school receptionist, coming into the classroom, walking up to the teacher who was sitting behind her desk, whispering something into her ear and then both of them looking in my direction. The teacher asks me to pack my stuff away and take it all with me as I am requested to see the head teacher in her office. As any school student across the world would no doubt ascertain, being suddenly summoned to the head teacher's office is hardly ever for positive reasons. I slowly pack my bag, at the same time trying to rack my brains as to why the head teacher might want to see me. In the end, I figure it must be because the previous week we had had a literature test and my score was not outstanding, it was in fact uncharacteristically low. I give a sigh of relief thinking, yes, that is what it must be all about and already make a mental plan of how I'd reassure her that I will study harder for the next test.

I follow the receptionist to the head teacher's office. She knocks softly on the door, slowly opens the door hesitantly and ushers me in. The office is fairly large with a freshly waxed parquet floor in the middle of which a beautiful, eye catching rug, possibly Persian, is placed. The room seems slightly dim as the only light is the natural light coming in from the windows overlooking an exquisite garden featuring a few incredibly majestic oak and almond trees as well as some of the most brightly coloured flowers, almost reminiscent of a Japanese garden. As soon as I walk into the office, I notice the head teacher standing in front of her huge, imposing walnut desk, behind which, on the wall, proudly hangs a picture of the president Ceausescu next to a full length Romanian flag. I feel a little intimidated being here, in this room, in the presence of the head teacher, not least because I am not overly fond of her. Every time I lock eyes on her, I can't help but think of my grandmother's voice at the back of mind. "Ha! That woman probably doesn't have an education beyond high school and she calls herself a head teacher! She made head teacher thanks to not any other skill or knowledge, beyond licking communist ass. See that damn pin she always wears on the lapel of her suit blazer? That shows her true colours alright! Her loyalty is not to the education of children in this country but to the Communist Party! Communist scum, that's what she is!"

As I stand here in front of her, I yet again hear my grandmother's voice in my head, and I can't help but half smile to myself as I shyly walk closer to where she is stood. And while doing so, I am surprised to notice out of the corner of my eye, that there are three other men to the side of her, somewhat in the shadows, hence why I hadn't seen them straight away upon entering the office. They are all wearing three quarter length, dark coats over their suits and they all seem to be staring at me peculiarly. I also notice that one is holding in his hand what looks like rolled up magazines whilst another one has his hands behind his back, as if hiding something – or perhaps just holding his briefcase.

This entire unexpected set up adds to my already heightened sense of nervousness and in order to hide it, I smile a little as I gently nod my head in their direction, as a means to greet them. The eerie stillness of the situation is brutally interrupted by the head teacher, who by way of greeting me, starts shouting at the top of her voice, one hand on her hip, the other hand outstretched, finger pointing accusingly and menacingly at me.

"What the hell do you have to smile about? Wipe that smirk right off your face!"

I am taken aback, shocked even, as despite having had little contact with her over the years, whenever I would come across her she would always get out of her way to be pleasant, amicable even, whilst enquiring about how I was progressing at school and always finishing off with, "Please make sure you let your father know that I have enquired about your welfare and how you're getting on here, at school."

Now this very same woman standing across the room from me, is screaming threateningly at me…

I must look puzzled by what seems to me to be an uncharacteristic and uncalled for outburst, for one of the men standing next to her clears his throat, steps forward in front of the head teacher, in what appears to be like a protective manner of her, and sternly says, "So, pupil Baleanu, your highly esteemed head teacher here has had to learn, in a very short space of time, some very ugly and vile truths about you," the disgust in his voice loud and clear. He narrows his eyes looking at me and a sly, malicious smirk forms on his lips at the look of shock and indignation on my face.

A softly spoken, "Oh?" is all I can manage, as I can feel my throat tightening and my heart pounding in my chest.

"Yes," he continues as if he's just warming up on the subject, "it so seems that unbeknown to her, your highly esteemed head teacher has been harbouring a disgusting traitor among her exemplary pupils, a traitor who managed to sneak her way right under the head teacher's nose!" he finishes off with a high screech. He pauses and I look at him silently, trying to work out why he is sharing this information with me. Does he think that I might know them, this traitor? Then, he picks up from where he left off. "But of course, you know all about that, don't you?" he looks at me with raised eyebrows as if expecting an answer but I frown and shake my head whilst remaining silent for I am too terrified to open my mouth. I don't have a clue what he is talking about.

"Don't you, I said! Speak up for all of us to hear you!" he shouts, leaping towards me until we're almost nose to nose, voice raised and finger pointing in my face, in the same manner the head teacher had done a few moments earlier.

"No, I don't! I don't know what you are talking about!" I stammer nervously in defence, tears stinging my eyes. My heart is now beating so fast it feels like deafening thuds, while my knees are wobbling so violently I am afraid I might collapse any second now. I can feel my hands sweating and shaking too, so in an effort to hide them from view, I cross my arms and dig my nails in the sides of my upper arms in order to calm myself down, to give myself something else to focus on, to keep myself from crying or falling down. Seeing this gesture, the man who had just been talking to me, and who for the past few seconds had begun pacing slowly in front of me, jumps straight up in front of me, yet again so close that I can smell the stench of cigarettes on his breath, and he violently jerks my arms down, on either side of me.

"You stand up straight in front of us, pupil Baleanu," he thunders so loudly that my ears start ringing. "Does it look like we are here for a friendly chat?"

A few seconds of silence ensue which feel like an eternity. I wish my mum or my grandma were here with me, as I feel so alone and vulnerable, but I try my hardest to hide my fear from them as I suspect that they might be using it as proof that

I might be guilty of something rather than being innocent, which of course, I know I am.

As I stand there, speechless, looking at them all, a second man, the one who seemed to me like he was holding some rolled up magazines in his hand as I walked in, steps forward. As he does so, the man who had previously been talking to me, walks back into the shadows and falls in line with the head teacher and the other man, the one who is holding the case behind his back.

This man, the one with the rolled up magazines in his hand, is quite short with a bit of a pot belly, a small black moustache and slick black hair combed back. He gently walks forward, towards me, stops a few paces away from me, looks at me in disgust and for a second, given the expression on his face, I feel like he might spit at me. Instead, he throws whatever he is holding in his hand at my face and my chest. I close my eyes and put my hands up instinctively and take a step back. I steady myself and look on the floor around me. An array of pop and fashion magazines are scattered at my feet. I look at them curiously because I recognise them to be some of my very own cherished magazines, the ones I love reading and re-reading and sharing with my friends and which my father would bring back from work on a regular basis in order for me to keep up with British culture…

I'm lost in thought and not quite taking in what the man is saying, though I can see his lips moving, when I see him as if in slow motion, twisting his hand in a fist and suddenly punching me with it, right in the pit of my stomach. I double up in pain and gasp for air. The pain of the punch had gone right through me, for it feels like my entire body had been hit with the punch, not just my stomach. I feel like screaming though nothing but silent gasps of air come out and now, I can't help the tears spilling from my eyes.

"…Been spreading western propaganda, trying to indoctrinate children with your sick, twisted, demented beliefs and enemy ideology! Even going as far as sharing images of pornography with them, trying to corrupt our innocent youngsters!" I have somehow managed to somewhat regain my composure a little, despite the pain, but upon hearing his words I feel like I'd been hit all over again. I can't help but stare at him in disbelief, mouth and eyes wide open. I want to scream, to shout at the top of my lungs. "Why are you saying these things to me? It is not true! None of it is true!" But instead the only thing that comes out of my now dry mouth is a weak, barely audible whisper of "Not true". This proves a little too much for this little moustached man, who all of a sudden becomes crazed with rage.

"It is not true?" he screams in my face. "What is not true?" he continues. "Is it not true that you have been sharing information from these vile, sick, western propaganda magazines with other children from this school?" he looks at me enquiringly. I don't know how to answer this question as indeed me and my friends, many of whom are at the same school as me, had spent hours poring over these magazines, looking at pop stars' pictures, trying to copy their style or learning the lyrics of different Madonna or Kylie songs by heart. Is that what this man meant when he said that I was spreading western propaganda? I wonder to myself. Surely not, as it was my father who had given me those and he had been given these magazines at work. I always thought that if it was OK for him to read them and share them with me and mum, then it would never be a problem, me sharing the magazines with my friends. And just like that, I start to feel petrified at the thought that sharing these magazines might now be the cause of problems for my father at work. How stupid of me to share them with others! My father will be so furious with me, now! I feel so stupid and reckless! I'm sure he will now never allow me to even peek at one, ever again!

"...And as for sharing pornographic material, you will go to prison for that!" I now hear the man say as if in a foggy, bad dream I can't wake up from. At hearing the word pornography associated with me, my cheeks start burning, feeling like they are on fire with shame and embarrassment.

"It is not true," I protest again, weakly and faintly in less than a whisper for fear of not angering him.

"It's not true?" he shouts in my face, then crouching down, going through some of the magazines in front of me, before grabbing a copy of Vogue magazine, leafing through it and opening it at a particular page. He turns the magazine round so that the page is right in front of my eyes.

"What do you call this?" he asks, pounding on the page with his fist. I look at the picture and see a model showcasing a golden bikini swimsuit. *Why?* I think to myself. *This is the very magazine my neighbour friend and I were looking at just last night after I dropped my mum's bag off there.* I swear I had left this magazine at my friend's house with her mum because her mum wanted to choose an outfit for me to make for her in time for Christmas! *How did this man get this magazine?* I ask myself, completely puzzled.

I open my mouth trying to say something but nothing comes out. I want to say to him, this is not pornography, this is just a girl wearing a bikini suit just like I do every summer at the beach and just like my mum does and no doubt your daughter and wife and possibly your mum do, too. But no words come out and as I stand there, desperately trying to fight off the tears at the injustice and unfairness of it all, the man leaps forward, spits at my face and slaps me hard across the face. For one second, I think that side of my face has literally caught fire, it burns so hot. And even though I don't want to, for the second time this afternoon, tears start streaming down my face as my chin starts trembling uncontrollably. I wipe the tears off quickly with the back of my hand, hoping that this is now going to be the end of this, whatever this is; that I'd had my punishment and that I would be now allowed to go home where I desperately want to be.

However, it is not to be. Because just as the short man with the moustache walks back into the shadows where the three others are stood silently, watching the events unfolding, the third man steps forward. He is tall and quite thin, maybe the same age as my father; though unlike my father, his hair is already almost completely grey, and he is wearing a pair of gold rimmed glasses. I watch him nervously and on guard, not knowing what to expect as he slowly walks towards me. He stops a few steps in front of me and holds forward in the space between us, what he was hiding all this time behind his back.

He speaks calmly, though his tone betrays a nasty and mean streak.

"And this? What do you know about this?" he asks me.

I look at it for a few seconds even though I had recognised it straight away, from the very first glance. The burgundy hold-all bag. The one which my mother had given me the previous evening to take to my friend's house and which indeed I had done as requested. I look at it, but I say nothing, yet in my head, I wonder if my friend had indeed alerted them to it – because otherwise how would these people had got to know about its existence? It doesn't make any sense, though, because my friend took such little interest in it when I dropped the bag off with her. Hadn't even looked inside it in my presence…

This third, tall man starts talking and I listen intently even though my head is spinning with countless questions, my cheek still feels hot from the earlier slap and my stomach still feels the impact from the blow received.

"Stolen goods, that's what this is! Which you have been trying to hide! That's another prison sentence right here!" he says calmly with a sly self-satisfied smile, as if gloating.

I stand quiet, head bowed, as I listen to him speak, and then the words 'prison sentence' start to register. I think of my little sister and how if I'd be sent to prison I would not be able to see her again, which fills me with panic and unbearable sorrow. At the same time the thought of not seeing her again, jolts me into defending myself for I do not want to ever be separated from my little sister, ever again, especially for something that was not true.

"These are not stolen goods, these are my grandma and great-grandma's jewellery. I don't know what my friend told you, but if you ask my mum she would tell you the truth!" I say by way of justifying their belonging. The man looks at me and sniggers, half turns to look at those present behind him, who also start to snigger patronisingly.

"This jewellery does not belong to your grandparents. They were bought by your father for your mother with the salary given to him by our great, esteemed communist state. This jewellery belongs to the state and you were trying to steal it, to hide it away from us!" he concludes, staring me in the eye.

"No!" I shout, shaking my head in protest, feeling an intense rage inside. I had never known my father to ever buy my mother any jewellery though my mother and grandmother would regularly share my grandma's or her mother's jewels for special occasions. "There are photos in our house, in our family photo albums of my grandmother and great-grandmother wearing these jewellery even before I was born, before my parents got together, before my mum even met my dad…" I try to explain before the tall man before me lounges forward and punches me to the side of the head, grabs me by the arm and roughly drags me after him, towards the door. I feel dizzy and uncertain on my feet, following the unexpected blow to the head, so I stagger behind him as he pulls me along. He opens the doors and violently throws me out, where despite trying my hardest to maintain my balance, I stumble and fall to the ground, just outside of the head teacher's office door.

"Go home now, we've heard enough of your lies for the moment. We'll deal with you properly at a later date!" I hear him say behind me as he slams the door shut.

I feel dizzy and disoriented, and there's a ringing in my ear on the side of the head where I had been hit, but the moment the door closes behind him, there is only one thought that crosses my mind, *I need to get to my little sister.* I don't want anyone to harm her and I dread to think that she might be taken and subjected to the same kind of treatment I had just been in myself, for some kind of trumped up injustice. She is only six years old and I'd be damned if I will allow any harm to come to her. So I swiftly pick myself up, do my best to shake the dizziness and confusion off and force myself to focus on hurrying to my little sister's classroom. Once there, I unceremoniously throw the classroom door open, I burst in without a word, to see all the children stood quietly behind their chairs, no doubt awaiting to be dismissed for the end of school day. In which case, I must have been in the head teacher's office for more or less one hour, from the start of my maths lesson until the end of the school day. I frantically look around and spot my little sister standing towards the back of the class. I quickly walk up to her, scoop her up in my arms, pick up her bag and run out of the door with her. The teacher looks at me bewildered, opens her mouth as if she is about to say something but then it looks like she changes her mind. The end-of-day bell goes just as we are half running and half walking out of the school gate.

All the way home my mind keeps racing between thoughts of telling my mum what had happened in the head teacher's office and therefore finding some comfort and maybe even an explanation for it all, and thoughts of angering my mum with what I would tell her. What if she will be really cross with me for sharing the magazines with my friends? I ask myself. But then, she never said that I couldn't... What if she gets angry when I have to tell her that I'd lent my friend her Vogue magazine without telling her so? But wasn't she the one to always say that I needed all the possible practice to master my clothes making skills, to fit all different shapes and sizes? And finally the thought that upset me the most – *What will she say or do, when I tell her that the hold-all bag she entrusted me with, the one that...what did she say? Oh, yes, that 'one day we might have to depend upon it for our survival', was now in the possession of someone else. Someone else who? Oh no!* How can I explain to her who those men even were? I wasn't entirely sure myself! It felt like they were officials. But, were they government officials? Didn't they say something like, 'Your father bought the jewellery with the state salary, so therefore the jewellery is actually ours'? Perhaps they were government officials after all. But then again, perhaps not... Oh no, my mum would be so mad at me, that's for sure!

We are getting closer to approaching the house, but even before we get to walk through the door I realise that something's wrong. Very, very wrong. For what seems like every single person from the surrounding and neighbouring buildings are looking out of their windows, muttering and staring in the direction of our house. And now, upon noticing us, some are staring, nudging, pointing and whispering to each other as me and my little sister are walking past, under their windows, towards our house. Just as we reach the front of our house, I look up and notice that every single light in every single room of the house is switched on. Through the open windows I see the head tops of what looks like a swarm of men in every room, going from one corner to another, one side to the other…

Hesitantly, we walk up to the entrance, and I notice that the front door is wide open though even before I see it, I hear my mother's imposing voice shouting, "Put that fridge down, right now! Put it back where you found it! Now!"

As I inch closer, I spot two men about to carry our fridge out of the front door. I move out of the way, to one side, and a second later my mum appears right beside them, grabbing at one of the men's shirt, finger pointing to where the fridge used to live.

"That fridge was bought by my father. I have the receipt to prove it, so bring it back and place it back where it belongs, straight away! I have children who still need feeding, you know, and if I no longer have any rights then I'm sure as hell that they still do," my mum aggressively tells them. The men stop, look at each other and for a brief moment they seem unsure as to what to do next. They also seem weighted down by the heavy load and so they momentarily put the fridge down. My mum then disappears in the living room for a few seconds, only to return holding an A4 sheet of paper which she thrusts in the two men's faces.

"There!" she points at something on the paper. "The brand of the fridge, the model, the series, the price, paid for by my father. His name and signature right there!" The men look at the piece of paper, at each other and then shrug their shoulders in uncertainty.

"Now bring it back to where you found it!" my mum orders them. One of the men gives the other a nod, they both crouch down at the same time, lift the fridge off the floor and take it back into the kitchen.

My sister and I walk into the hallway of our house and my mum looks at us as if she doesn't really see us. It seems that she hasn't even registered our presence and she is looking straight through us. I help my sister take her coat and shoes off and we walk into what seems like a house under occupation. There are tens of strange, unknown faces of men in every single room, opening, moving, even dislodging pieces of furniture and even light fittings.

In the midst of all this chaos and confusion, my mum, my grandma and even my 85 year old great-grandma who lives with us, are frantically going from one room to another and from one group of men to another, telling them not to touch anything that had been bought and paid for by my maternal grandparents and for which they have the paperwork, the receipts to prove it. There are raised voices of protest that can be heard in every corner of the house, some male, some female, but my sassy 85-year-old great-grandmother's is the one that is the thickest with attitude.

"What are you doing?" I can hear her saying to some of the men and half see her through the crack of her bedroom door. "You want to take my bed away? What are you going to do with a bed that's 30 years old? Crazy communists! Crazy, filthy, uneducated communists! Yes, you heard me right, stop staring! What you going to do? Lock me up and pay for my care fees for the rest of my days because I call it as I see it? Yes, I'm glad he's defected! Ha! And I'm glad he's stung you idiots as he so obviously has! The only thing I'm not glad about is that he's waited for so long to do it…"

I almost gasp in surprise and shock, at my great-grandmother's words. For finally, this somewhat clarifies to me what is happening and reason behind it. So, that was it. My father had defected. I knew what the word meant for I had heard it used by my mother in the many arguments my parents would have over the past months. When I asked my grandma at the time, about it, she had said that I cannot say what I heard to anyone else because I'd get into trouble and get my parents into trouble, too. She did eventually explain to me that it meant leaving your job and possibly your country for good in favour of somewhere else. Even when my grandma said that using that word publicly would get me into trouble, I didn't quite understand the implications of it, though I was certainly starting to, now…

I walk away from my great-grandma's bedroom door and try to find my mum among all this bedlam. I walk from one room to another, trying to avoid stepping on scattered drawers, clothes, papers, until I see her. She is stood in the middle of the dining room, arms crossed, head held up high, defiantly, talking to a few men who had taken over our dining room table, piles of paper in front of each one and right in the centre of the table, about three or four drawers that I recognise to have come from my parents' bedroom.

One of the men, the one sat at the head of the table, puts down some papers, takes his glasses off, looks over at my mum and says to her, "So, you're telling us that nothing in this house was bought by Vergil?"

My mother looks him in the eye, sighs and calmly replies, "The telly, the VCR and this ugly rug underneath this table," she says pointing at the rug under the dining room table. "That is all he's ever contributed to in this house. You're welcome to them. So, take them and get out of here, together with your herd."

The man looks up from the paperwork he had become engrossed in again, and raises one eyebrow, with an amused look on his face. "Not quite ready yet," he replies slowly. "We still have to fully establish what truly belongs to us and what still rightfully belongs to you."

My mum glances over at the paper which the man had been looking at and is now placing on top of the pile in front of himself. She raises an eyebrow herself and asks seemingly innocently, "My husband's degree certificate belongs to you?"

"It does," the man replies seriously. "He studied at the expense of the Romanian communist state and was awarded the degree by the Romanian communist state as all degrees are," he explains while pointing at the crest at the top of the certificate. "So technically, his degree and therefore, this certificate, belongs to the state. Given the circumstances, it now needs to be returned to the state," the man says looking gleefully triumphant at my mum.

My mum stares at him in silence for a few seconds and we both watch him as he picks up another piece of paper, this time my father's birth certificate, which he also places on top of the pile in front of him.

"Did the state give birth to him, as well?" my mum can't resist asking, a small sarcastic smile forming on her lips. I'm stood right next to my mum and upon hearing her remark I can't help letting out a giggle. The man furiously looks up at me and then at my mother. He is about to say something but he is interrupted by the arrival of the three men I had encountered earlier at my school. Upon seeing them and recalling the events of earlier in the afternoon, I freeze to the spot.

"Evening, boss," they all say to the man with whom my mum had just had the exchanges. The man looks at them somewhat puzzled as if he wasn't actually expecting to see them there. One of the three men walks up to the man he had just called 'boss' and whispers something in his ear. As he does so, the boss man's eyes linger upon me and then my mum for a few seconds. When he finishes whispering in his ear, the man goes back to stand in line with the two others as if awaiting orders.

"The family photo albums," the boss man finally says to my mum. "You need to give these gentlemen your family photo albums and then, you might want to take a seat and enlighten us as for how long you've know that Vergil was intending to defect."

My mum looks at him, dismayed look on her face, then at the three men who had just arrived and then back at him again. "The hell you want my family photos for?" she asks in disbelief. The man doesn't answer and my mum, arms crossed, feet apart, grounded on the floor, has obviously no intention of moving. The 'boss' man dismisses the three men with a wave of the hand asking them to go look for the photos themselves, without looking up from another piece of paper he is studying. Eventually, after a short silence, he resumes the conversation.

"So, Gina, how long have you know that he was going to defect?" he asks again.

My mum waits a few seconds, studies his face, looks out of the window and then replies, "How do you even know that he's defected? What if he's been taken ill and he's in some hospital over there? Or maybe got run over and laying dead by the side of the road somewhere?" she asks.

"Mmm…that would no doubt, be preferable for both you and us. But we have it on good authority that he defected. Our concern now is to establish how much you know about all of this, how long you've known it for, and to what extend you are implicated in all of this," he concludes.

My mum walks over to him, leans across the table so that her face is level with his and stares him in the eye. "Well, I can tell you right now that I know nothing of it and I am not implicated, as you called it, in anything what so ever. Now, take your herd of idiots and get the fuck out of my house!" and that being said, my mother turns around and goes into the kitchen to make herself some tea.

I can't remember precisely for how much longer these people continued to intrude in our house but eventually they all start to go, one group at a time. Darkness has fallen outside and eventually the house falls deadly quiet. And so we start to slowly inspect the damage. The TV, the VCR and dining room rug, all gone as are all of my father's documents, certificates and paperwork. Doors of wardrobes left open, drawers pulled out and their contents left scattered all over the floor of the house. In the bathroom, the bath panel had been removed and casually discarded to one side as had the toilet cistern. The house looked as if it had been burgled, disturbed and disarranged at every level. But, at the end of the day that was pretty much it.

"Mess can get tidied up," I say to my mum at which she mumbles, "Not this one. Not so quickly, this time."

We start tidying up and it is then that I realise that I hadn't had the chance to tell her about what had happened to me at school earlier in the day. So I now start to recount all of those events to her. She listens, blank expression on her face, staring into nothingness, until I finish telling her everything. Then she finally says, "That's why they took all of our photo albums. That was our evidence, our proof, that that jewellery doesn't belong to their state, that it had been in our family since way before your father became part of it. I was wondering why they wanted to take those photo albums…"

In the end we all go to bed, tired, drained, dejected, all with our own thoughts. I fall into a restless sleep where I dream that our house had caught fire and even though we manage to get out of it, we can't do anything else other than watch it burn down to the ground. The first of many similar dreams I start to experience.

Following the violation of our house under the pretence of seizing my father's belongings, my sister, my mum and I go about our daily business as if in a daze, neither my mum nor myself mentioning the incident thereafter. Or my father or anything related, for that matter. There is a deafening, heavy atmosphere in the house but at the same time, eventually, after a week or so, some sort of calm is restored. Soon enough, we even start to think that some kind of normality, of a new, different kind, is to be expected, with the worst now being behind us.

We have no news from or about my father, except for the snippet of information from the other day from the 'boss man' who had been leading the seizure of possessions, who had stated that he had it on good authority that my father was indeed alive and that he had defected. Besides this comment, we had no knowledge of his wellbeing, his whereabouts or if he was even dead or alive, or had truly defected.

Two more uneventful weeks go by. It's a dark winter's afternoon, with heavy, black clouds threatening a snow storm. It's the beginning of December, and my sister and I return from school one day to the sound of the phone ringing. My elderly great-grandma is probably in her bedroom and thus unable to hear it. So, at the sound of it, I rush into the house and run to answer the phone.

"Diana, is that you, sweetie?" I hear a female voice which I don't recognise straight away. "It's Mrs Pancea, I'm the receptionist at your mum's place of work…" It sounds like either the line is crackling or her voice is breaking. I try to put a face to the name and I vaguely remember my mother introducing me some time ago to someone by that name at her place of work. "Your mama…" she carries on as if carefully choosing her words, "she wanted me to assure you that she'll be back home as soon as she can…"

"Oh?" I answer, puzzled as to why she would get someone else to tell me that, why wouldn't she pick up the phone and tell me herself. "Why is that? Where is she?" I ask the receptionist, at the same time flicking the lights on in the room so that my little sister, on her way to her bedroom, can see where she's going.

"Don't get too upset, sweetie," she continues saying. Though of course, upon hearing her say these words, an inner panic alarm starts to ring and my breathing almost stops. "…but she has been taken. By a couple of men. They told her to take her coat and bag because…" she drifts off, as if unsure whether to carry on or not.

"Because what?" I ask, trying to sound calm but my voice betraying me, as panic has now completely taken over.

"Because, she's under arrest and there are questions that they need answers to," she starts talking really fast now, almost as fast as my breathing has now become. "They wouldn't allow her to call you, she asked them to allow her to speak to you, but they said there's no time for that. They marched her out of the building, by her arms, but she managed to quickly shout at me to call you and let you know she'd be home as soon as she can. So that you don't worry…" she says by means of ending.

So that I don't worry? I think to myself. *I feel sick with worry. Literally.* I have no idea where my mum has been taken, why, by whom and for how long… "Where did they take her, do you have any idea?" I finally ask the receptionist.

"I'm sorry, sweetie. I don't know. They put her in the back of their car and sped off. That's all I know."

Tears start running down my face and I can't help letting out a quiet sob. The receptionist is speaking again but I'm no longer listening, so I put the phone down, too distraught to even say goodbye. I feel like raging, like screaming, like throwing the phone across the room in pain and frustration but, over my shoulder, I see my little sister standing in the doorway, her big eyes staring at me.

"What's wrong?" she asks worried, and I know that I have to keep it together for her sake. So I swallow hard, wipe the tears from my eyes and simply say,

"Mum has to work late tonight, baby girl, so she won't be back until really late."

I muster a smile and go over to her to give her a big hug. We go into the kitchen where I make her some warm milk and give her a biscuit. I decide to firstly call my grandma to speak to her and tell her what's happened. Then, I would need to go see my great-grandma and tell her, too, what I learned, what had just happened to my mum.

I call my grandma's number but there's no answer. I wait a few minutes, fuss nervously over my sister a little and then call again. Still no answer. I look at the time. 5 pm. Strange. Even though my grandma is quite the social butterfly, she doesn't like leaving her house once it's dark, so her friends flock mainly at her place in the afternoon or early evening. Still, it's not that late so, perhaps, she is still at someone's house. I'll try again in a short while.

I desperately want to quiet, to drown the worried thoughts crossing my mind, so I switch the radio on as we no longer have a TV, having being seized by the state the other week. My mind then drifts to happier times and places as I listen to a song for a few minutes before I register the presenter's voice and realise that he's talking in English. Damn! BBC World Service. I quickly jump up and attempt to turn off the radio which is met with a whine of protest from my sister. In the past, as a family we would regularly listen to BBC World Service, Voice of America or Radio Free Europe, when my father was still with us. He would always half joke that if anyone was to overhear us doing so, we would all possibly go to prison, regardless of his, or his father's position. But now with my father gone this is not even half a joke, so I quickly change the frequency before anyone overhears and I put myself at risk.

I try my grandma's number again. Still no answer, so I go to see my great-grandma, up in her bedroom. She is sat in an armchair beside a floor lamp, reading a book. I can see that my sister has already made her way to our great-grandma's room, as she is now sat at a small desk drawing in a book. I sit down on the edge of her bed, a beautiful blanket, embroidered in gorgeous, vibrant colours, covering her bed. She puts her book down and senses that everything is not as it should be. So, she nudges closer to me and takes my hand in hers. I tell her in a quiet voice, because I don't want my little sister to overhear me and get upset, what I had learned about my mum. Even though I try really hard not to cry, the tears can't stop falling down my face. My great-grandma gets her handkerchief out of her bathrobe pocket and gently wipes my face with it. It smells of jasmine and the smell alone makes me feel a bit better. My great-grandma gives me a kiss on the head and tells me,

"Don't let these bastards cower you. Don't let them beat you down. That's what they want. Because they're scared. They're scared of the truth, they're scared of what people really believe of them and they are scared of the change that's coming their way. Their only power comes from instilling fear. And that's why they are now lashing out because they want to see us fearful, defeated, dejected, giving up completely. But we won't do that! Not us, not ever! We are strong and smart, though women – all five of us: you, your sister, your mum, your grandma, me. We have each other and we will do what we do best – we will fight, we will stand up to them and we will face whatever life brings us. Because we can take it. And we will take it with strength, dignity and integrity. Something which these communist beasts lack. And eventually, when there will be so many other people no longer being able to hold the pain inside, ready to stop living in fear and to shout out the truth, they, these beasts, will no longer be able to silence it and justice will come to light. It's the way of the universe. No one can defy that. No one can prevent it from happening, not even the communists."

I look at her, into her eyes, and despite her 85 years of age, I feel so invigorated by her strength, by her resilience, by her calm determination.

I watch her as she slowly and painfully gets up, saying that she needs to go cook dinner for us all now, when I can hear the phone ringing. I get up and quickly run down to get it, convinced it would be my grandma.

"Hello? Is this Nelly's daughter?"

Damn! Not my grandma! I don't recognise the voice but it sounds as if it belongs to an elderly woman.

"No, it's Diana, Nelly's granddaughter," I reply. "My mum is not home yet," I add quickly.

"Oh…" she hesitates before she adds, "I was with your grandma earlier at her place. Do you know when your mum will be back? Or where I can find her? I have something to tell her…" I can hear the urgency in her voice, but of course I don't know when my mum will be back and I have no intention of sharing with this woman whom I don't even know, the current whereabouts of my mother's.

"Mum is not available for the time being," is all I volunteer, vaguely. "Is my grandma alright? Do you know where she might be now, because I've been trying to reach her at her place, but I'm not getting any answer?" I ask quickly, eager for any information, before she might put the phone down.

"Well, that's why I wanted to speak to your mum, you see…but you sound like you're old enough to be trusted with passing the message on to your mum," she concludes and I don't argue with her.

"I was with your grandma earlier, like I was saying," she resumes talking, "when these two nasty characters turned up at her place, rang the doorbell non-stop until she got there to open it. I mean what manners...then, when she opened the door, they barged right past her, walked straight into the living room, like they were the ones who owned the place. They looked around, stared at us for a few seconds, we were in the middle of a card game... Anyway, they told her to get a coat as she had to go with them, but didn't say where or why. Poor Nelly, she was frightened, I could tell, but she put her coat on and told them, 'I'm ready, let's not waste any more time.' She asked me to lock up for her before they all walked out of the place..."

I didn't need nor want to hear anymore. I knew straight away where they must have taken my grandma, probably same place as my mum, presumably for the same reason... I hear my grandma's friend's voice again, "I mean, I don't know who these men were, but I figured some officials. I'm sure it must be some misunderstanding. Your mum will be able to sort it out and clarify the situation. I mean, poor Nelly..." she continues, but, for the second time this evening, I put the phone down as I no longer want to listen to the words being said at the other end of the line.

I run to the kitchen, where my great-grandma is now cooking us dinner, and I blurt out, "They've taken Mutti, too. What if they come and get you, too, Mammy? What will I do, here, all by myself with Anna? And if they take me, too, what would happen to Anna?" I ask sobbing, barely breathing, overwhelmed by a feeling of dread. My great-grandma looks at me and hands me a glass of warm milk.

"There, there. Stop crying. Don't you worry, they won't take me. I will refuse!" she finally says firmly. "I'll just plonk myself down on the sofa and refuse to move. What will they do? Carry me away? I'm too heavy for one person, even two people to carry me!" she says and she is right, she is a rather heavy lady. "What else would they do? Bring in a crane?" she chuckles and despite the seriousness of the situation, we both start to laugh at the image of my great grandma being whisked away by crane.

Shortly after, my little sister comes into the kitchen, we have dinner, the three of us, I do a bit of homework with my sister and then it's time to put her to sleep. I lay down next to her in bed and hope that I might fall asleep, too, but how can I? I can't stop thinking about my mum and my grandmother, their whereabouts, if they are alright and when they might be coming home. I wonder if they are together in the same place or in separate places. If they even know that the other one had been taken. If they're hungry, if they might have been given some dinner or even something to drink. Every time I hear a car or a noise outside, I jump up and look out of the window, thinking that it might be them. But every time I'm left disappointed.

I drift in and out of a light, fretful sleep when I finally hear the engine of a car coming to a stop right underneath my window. I look at the alarm clock next to me – it's 2 am. I sit up, rub my eyes for a second and look out of the window. I see my mum, slowly and gently helping my grandma out of a taxi. Thank goodness, they're home! And they are safely together. I get out of the bed in a rush, quickly grab and throw a bathrobe on and run to open the front door, feeling relieved and jubilant. I turn the lock and open the door, wide smile of anticipation on my face, ready to throw my arms around them and jump and down with glee when I'm stopped dead in my tracks.

There is nothing that could have prepared me for the sight before me. The look of utter shock must be clearly etched on my face. My mum looks at me for a split second, before whispering, "Make room, get inside the house and close the door right now!"

It is my mum I see first as she is leading the way, slowly pulling along my grandma's arm with a gentle encouragement of, "C'mon, ma, one more step. One more step..." I can only see one side of my mum's head and the hair is all matted by mud and dirt which is also on the side of her face and her cream coat, too.

I hear my grandma's soft whimpering before I actually see her face properly. A whimpering which she lets out with every step, as a small child who is hurt. When they cross the threshold, I come face to face with my grandma when they walk past me. I involuntarily give out a gasp and my mouth opens in absolute shock, disbelief and pain. Half of my grandma's face is so swollen, her left eye is closed shut. Above her left eye, there is a one-inch cut which is still gushing with blood, dripping down her face and onto her coat. Even though her coat is dark navy, I can see where the dripping blood has been staining it, shining a dark crimson colour. They both walk into the kitchen, side by side, my mum still gently pulling her mum along whilst whispering soothingly. My mum then helps grandma into an armchair and as she does so she half turns to say to me over her shoulder, "Bring me one of your sharp sewing needles and some white thread."

I quickly run into my bedroom, pull out a chair, jump onto it and look for a needle in my sewing box which is on top of my wardrobe, out of my little sister's reach. I look at my little sister sleeping so peacefully and I pray to God that she doesn't wake up to see mum and grandma in their current state. I quietly close the door behind me and return to the kitchen, where my mum is now handing my grandma some pills and helping a glass of water to her lips. She then opens a kitchen cupboard door and gets out a small metal dish which she fills with water, places over the hob and then turns the hob on. I look back at my grandma. Her face is so white and still, I wonder for a split second if she's still alive. But I tell myself off the second the thought crosses my head as I don't want to entertain such energy. I hand my mum the needle with the thread through it, which she drops into the metal dish and I go to stand next to my grandma. I take her hand in mine. She tries to turn her head to look at me and even attempts what must be smile, however the pain proves too much and it comes across as a grimace.

"Make us some tea," Mum instructs me. "I'm going to scrub my hands and find some surgical gloves." She sounds tired, exhausted, her voice hoarse and her eyes bloodshot. I look at her, now that the other side of her face is turned my way and I notice that her lip is also cut, though the cut is nowhere as shocking or as deep as my grandma's eyebrow gush. She walks past me with a limp and as she does so, I notice that her tights, below the edge of her skirt, are ripped and that her legs are covered in a mixture of blood and mud. I have so many questions but dare not ask one.

I make the tea, keeping one eye on my grandma who is now whimpering softly again, in her armchair, head against the headrest, both eyes shut. The water in my mum's steel dish has also come to boil but I'm unsure as whether to switch the gas off or not so it carries on boiling.

Not before long, my mum returns and switches it off. I see she is also carrying a bag of disposable gloves, a small bottle of medicinal spirit, a pair of scissors and some cotton wool. Due to her medical training, my mum has always been more than capable of looking after mine and my sister's minor injuries at home and for that purpose she keeps a well-stocked bathroom cabinet. I watch as mum takes a sip of her tea and she brings the other cup I made, to grandma's lips, to help her take a sip. Then, she places the cup down and starts talking to my grandma, "Ma, this will hurt like hell now, but I've got to do it, you know that…" My grandma lets out a louder whimper, as if in protest, but then she becomes quiet, as if in defeat.

"Go wash your hands really well with soap and hot water and then don't touch anything. Come right back," she says to me and I do as I'm told.

When I return, my mum is already putting on a pair of gloves and she nods to me to do the same. She gets hold of some cotton wool and dabs some of the surgical spirit on it. I look at my grandma and notice that she is now holding my mum's skirt belt in her hands, a thick black leather one.

"I've got to do this ma or else you'll get an infection and God forbid you might lose your eye. Get ready now. C'mon. Bite down on that belt."

My grandma slowly takes the belt to her mouth and weakly puts it between her teeth. My mum waits for her to do so and then I see my mum dabbing quickly and efficiently at her mother's gush with one hand whilst holding her head steady with the other. My grandmother lets out an agonising but stifled cry and for a second, I'm certain my little sister will be awoken by it. My mum is quick and before long all the blood has been cleaned off to reveal a deep cut which is still giving out fresh blood. After mum becomes satisfied that the wound is clean, she throws in the bin the cotton wool, takes her gloves off, throws them in the bin, too and goes to pour some more white spirit over her hands. She flicks her hands dry and then grabs another pair of surgical gloves which she puts on.

"You need to get some cotton wool from here and dab some white spirit onto it, then wait till I tell you what to do," she tells me.

My hands are shaking and my knees are wobbling and I'm hoping, praying even, that she won't ask me to clean grandma's gush as I can't bear the thought of inflicting anymore pain on her. Meanwhile, my mum has taken the needle and thread from the silver dish and with a kick of her foot, placed a chair closer to my grandma.

"Right, here we go, ma, brace yourself," she tells her mum. But my grandma whimpers so softly I feel like she's already about to lose consciousness. Mum leans forward and with a quick and assured hand, starts stitching my grandma's wound. At first I can't watch and so I turn my head away as my grandma, still biting down on the belt, gives out stifled screams, but by the time my mum is done she is only whimpering softly.

My mum works fast, not taking into account any of my grandma's screams or whimpers as if she's completely shut everything out except for the job in hand. Just before she finishes, she asks me to wipe the blade of the scissors with the spirit and hand them to her. I sigh a sigh of relief and gratitude for it becomes obvious she doesn't expect me to inflict any pain on grandma. She cuts the thread, takes the belt from my grandma's lips and leans back on her chair, with a heavy sigh, "Done, ma. Try to sleep for a while. Do you want us to move you to a bed?" she asks her gently. My grandma gives the smallest shake of the head, so we decide to leave her in the armchair where she seems fairly comfortable.

My mum tidies the kitchen up, throwing all the used gloves, cotton wool and so on, in the bin.

"I'll try to get you some antibiotics from somewhere tomorrow, ma. I've got a doctor friend who might help us and get us some," she is still talking to my grandma, but my grandma has long since stopped responding, passed out in the armchair. Mum dims the light in the kitchen, looks at her mum for one last time to make sure that she's fairly comfortable and then picks up the scissors and spirit from the counter top and walks towards the bathroom. I follow her out of the kitchen, and make my way to my bedroom as I hear her say, "Go to bed now, it's late and you have school tomorrow."

I'm too exhausted to even answer her back. I get into my bedroom, notice that the clock states 3.20 am, fall onto the bed and cuddle up to my sister who is warm and soft and smells like honey like little children tend to smell. Before I know it, I start drifting to sleep to the sound of my mum turning the shower on in the bathroom.

At 7 am sharp the alarm goes off right next to my head. I look at the time and switch the alarm off, turning on the other side, feeling beyond exhausted and having no intention of getting up to go to school. My little sister is still sound asleep next to me so I try not to disturb her. A few moments later, I hear the alarm going off in my mother's bedroom, and before I know it she's popping her head round my bedroom door, saying, "Time to get up! You've got to get ready for school."

"I'm not going…" I groan in return. "I want to stay home today. I'm just too tired…" I add as means of an excuse, whilst remembering all of a sudden about my poor grandma and wondering how she might be feeling this morning.

"Oh, no, you are going to school! And you will do so, every single day, no matter what!" my mum snaps right back. "It's illegal for children to miss school and if you miss school, I'll be the one ending up getting arrested for it. And maybe you, too. So you will go to school, regardless of how tired you are, just like I will go to work," she says categorically.

"You're going to work today?" I ask in amazement and disbelief, given the ordeal of last night.

"I sure am. Because someone needs to earn money, to pay the bills, put food on the table. If I won't go in, they will use it as an excuse to get me fired. And we don't have the luxury of going through that."

I can't argue with that or my mother, for that matter, so I get up and go to the kitchen to see how my grandma is doing. But when I get there, I realise that she must have moved herself as the armchair is now empty. I go into the spare room, and there she is asleep on top of the bed, her clothes still on. I get a blanket from the wardrobe and cover her up, give her a gentle kiss on her cheek and notice that the swelling has somewhat subdued to be replaced by a reddish purplish colour. I go back to my bedroom and start getting myself ready whilst waking my sister up. I make us some breakfast, which we quickly shove down before running off to school.

The following days come and go pretty uneventfully, my mum's lip starts to heal and slowly there are signs of improvement in my grandma's wound and bruising, too. My mum did manage to get in touch with a doctor friend of hers who came to see my grandma the day following their arrests. She took a look at my grandma's stitches and asserted to us, "I couldn't have done a better job myself."

At which my mother replies, "I was afraid that if I'd take her to A&E, we would be wasting our time, that they would not treat her, you know, on their orders…" my mum adds as a means to justify as to why she didn't take her to the hospital that night.

My mum's doctor friend confirms her suspicions, "Without a doubt, they would have got the call not to administer any treatment. They would have made you wait for hours, fobbing you off with being busy. You did the right thing. Besides, you were probably gentler with her than any overworked A&E doctor would have been," she reassures my mum. My mum thanks her and for the course of antibiotics, too.

As they are walking to the front door, my mum asks her, "Aren't you scared they will find out you've helped us today? That you might suffer repercussions?"

"Ha!" her friend answers defiantly. "I'm a doctor. And I, unlike some others, I do remember swearing an oath to help others in need of medical care regardless of the situation. So those beasts can go and do one, for all I care!" My mum smiles and squeezes her arm in gratitude before saying goodbye.

After she closes the door behind her friend, mum turns to face me and says, "There are still some decent people left among evil…"

A false sense of normality starts to prevail yet again for a while, with all of us carrying on with our mundane tasks, work for mum, school for Anna and I, evenings spent reading a book, with my sister looking wistfully where the TV and VCR stood until a short while ago. We still have no news from my father and when I once mentioned to mum, "I hope Dad is OK. What do you think happened to him?" she frowns at me immediately and silently gesticulates to me to be quiet. I drop the matter immediately as I gather that she is afraid to talk openly on the subject in case our house is bugged.

As time passes, it becomes increasingly obvious that we are under surveillance, with one dark silver car constantly parked on the kerb in front of our house. Other cars come up to it at times and the men inside the car outside our house would swap with the newly arrived men, every few hours. At first, this was done discreetly with the changeover after we would switch the lights off for the night, but lately it is done quite openly, at any time of the day, regardless even whether any of us, in the family, might even be obviously watching them, out of the window.

My mum also mentions how she has started to notice a black car following her wherever she goes, literally kerb crawling alongside her as she makes her way to the bus stop and then following the bus, stopping behind it at every bus stop, for it to come to a standstill outside her place of work. "They might as well offer me a lift to work and back every day, since we are all going the same way," my mum jokes one day, when mentioning that she is still being followed around.

My grandma is on the mend, back on her feet, the bruising and swelling all but gone, except for a red, raging scar above her eye, a permanent reminder of that atrocious night. Then one night my mum gets back from work late, later than usual. Though at first I wasn't worried too much, given how it's winter, it's snowy and the public transport is even more unreliable at this time of the year, I know that something is not quite right the moment she walks through the door. The arm of her coat is all but hanging off, having come undone at the seams, her eyes are bloodshot and there is not one drop of make up on her face. All highly unusual for my mum given how much pride she takes in her appearance. She looks pale, vulnerable, exhausted. So weak, as if she's about to pass out. My grandma jumps up from the chair by the kitchen table where she is sat and runs towards her, trying to steady her.

"Gina, what's wrong? What happened? Come and take a seat!"

Mum sits down at the kitchen table and my grandma puts a cup of tea in front of her. Eventually, my mum slowly takes her coat off – which I make a mental note to mend and clean for her for the following day – she takes a few sips of the tea and starts talking.

"They took me in again, for questioning. This time they picked me up as I was walking to the bus stop, this morning. I tried to fight them off. But they just grabbed me right there in plain view of all the other people passing by. Everyone stopped and stared, mouths open to the floor. How humiliating! They grabbed, pulled me, and shoved me into the car. Again. Only that this time they took me to Calea Rahovei, not the usual police station."

"Ay, ay, ay!" my grandma lets out half a gasp, half a cry of terror. Although I'd never heard of the place, my grandma's reaction makes me believe it's no day spa.

"I've been there all day," my mum stops and puts her head in her hands for a few seconds. "I'm actually quite hungry," she says and my grandma starts putting something together as my mum continues her story. "Five different men, some of them people we know. They worked for Vergil. Like, you know, Danescu, Radulescu, Popescu…" and my grandma nods knowingly. "They took turns questioning me, taunting me, shouting, insulting me, spitting at me and…" she swallows hard, looks at me for a second and then looks away without finishing the sentence.

My grandma starts to cry quietly and goes to hug my mum, though my mum waves her off, stands up and says that she's tired, so she is going to take a shower and go to bed.

The following morning, my mum is up before me and I find her having a cup of coffee in the kitchen. She asks me to sit down with her for a minute. So, I sit down at the kitchen table, across from her.

"I've been thinking," she starts by saying, "I think that it will be for the best if you and Anna were to move to Mutti's house after Christmas. For a while, not for good, of course."

I open my mouth to object straight away at the thought of having what is left of our family split up once again. My mum, though, cuts me short, "No, listen, it's not healthy and it's not right for you and for Anna to live through all this…drama, this never ending…" she sighs as she can't find the appropriate word to describe the nightmare, the horror that has become her life and by extension our lives, too.

"Anyway, it will be just until things calm down. As Mammy says quite rightly so, 'nothing lasts forever'. And Mammy will go with you, to help look after you two. I need Mutti here, with me, because I'm afraid…" she pauses and I need to prompt her to finish off her thought.

"Well, I'm afraid that if Mutti is not here, they'll do something to get rid of me. Like stage a burglary in the middle of the night and just have me killed."

I start crying a little at hearing this, but my mum tries to put my mind at rest, "Stop crying. Like I said, I don't think they would do anything with Mutti here. A bit more difficult to justify two accidental deaths... I'm sorry, darling, but that's what the reality of our lives has come to..."

I sit up in stunned silence at the prospect of effectively having to fend by myself for my sister and me, and to an extent, for my elderly great-grandmother too, who is barely mobile. Also, stunned at the supposition that my mother is in so much danger that she is fearing for her life. Stunned at what our lives had become, how drastically they had changed over such a short period of time. It's been barely six weeks since my father's defection and life has changed so much I can barely recognise the life before that event.

After the Christmas holidays, which we spent uneventfully, mostly indoors, my sister, my great-grandma and myself, we move into Mutti's place, a flat in a block of flats right in the centre of Bucharest, some 10 km from my mum's house. The move proves to be so very difficult for my great-grandma and my heart breaks seeing how she bravely tries to climb the stairs with so much dignity, one by one and refusing any help. Eventually, we get there. We get into the flat, we settle in, Mutti promises to visit every other day and bring provisions, while we agree that my sister and I would visit mum and Mutti every weekend. It would be too onerous for my great-grandma to make the trip back to my mum's every weekend, but she insists that she will be perfectly fine with some needle work and a book to read when we are not there.

Both my sister and I start at a new school, which in many ways it's a relief. Nobody knows us, or about our history, so I quickly make new friends as does my sister. It's a joy to remember what it is like to be 14 again, chatting with friends, stopping for cake and lemonade or hot chocolate at the local café on our way back home from school, laughing, telling jokes, being silly for a change. I start to put at the back of my mind my father's defection, his absence, my mum and the ordeal through which, as far as I'm aware, she is still going through. For as much as her and Mutti try to protect me from details of it, I sometime overhear Mutti talking to her mum – my great-grandma – at times when we she comes with provisions, and it becomes obvious that my mother's arrests are becoming more and more frequent, more degrading, more violent.

I see it in my mother's physical appearance, too, when we go and visit at weekends. One time, she has a black eye which she tries to cover up from my sister and me, with makeup, but which I notice in the morning, before she has a chance to camouflage it. Another time, I catch a glimpse of bruises on her arm, her thigh, at the top of her back. But mainly, her now painfully thin frame is there for all to see, which makes my once strong and tough mum look so frail and helpless. Her eyes though, still tell a different story, one of rage mixed with outrage and defiance, though she doesn't verbalise it, not in our presence, anyway.

It is during one of our weekend visits that my mum approaches me one Sunday morning. She is hovering around me as if she's trying to say something but she's not quite sure how to start. In the end she just blurts it out, nervously, whilst doing the washing up, not looking at me while speaking.

"I've been given a summons. For you. From these bastard scumbags," which is how she has been referring to her tormentors from the very beginning. I sit still, frozen to the spot, not knowing how to respond, nor quite fully understanding the meaning of it.

"It says you need to present yourself at Calea Rahovei next Friday morning," she says as she rubs her hands dry on her apron and grabs out a flimsy piece of A5 paper from her trouser back pocket. She unfolds the paper and places it in front of me.

I look at it silently but it's all blurry as I can no longer control the tears streaming down my face. I think of the state of my grandma and my mum when they came home that night when they first got arrested. I also think of the whimper my grandma gave out when my mum had told her that they had started interrogating her at Calea Rahovei and the bruises on my mother's body that I've been noticing ever since then. Will the same fate await me? I feel petrified at the thought, but my mum interrupts my thoughts.

"C'mon, don't start now. You're just a child, they won't harm you…" she says trying to sound sobering, but her words lack conviction. I also think back to the encounter I had in the head teacher's office, the slaps and the punch to my stomach and I find no reassurance in her words.

"Besides, I'm coming with you. I'll be there with you all the way. And you won't have to answer any of their questions. Just say that you don't know what they're talking about. Which you will not, no doubt. They'll have to let you go in no time."

I ask myself with trepidation what kind of questions they might want to ask me and I say this much out loud, to my mother.

"They'll possibly want to know if you know any of the people that Dad knew, any foreign contacts whilst posted in London…"

I look at my mum puzzled and reply, "But he had lots of foreign contacts in London. That was his job, wasn't it?"

"Ha! Go figure!" my mum retorts. "And they might ask you some other things," she says pointing at the radio, but not putting it into words, yet again for fear of having our conversation tapped. I understand her meaning and remember when my father used to say that we'd all be potentially arrested if the authorities were to find out that we listened to Radio Free Europe, BBC World Service or The Voice of America, all of which we would all listen to, myself included, albeit looking at keeping up with the latest songs in the charts, but still…

"Just tell them you have no knowledge of anything and that will have to be that," my mum resumes her thought.

It's decided that I will go back to Mutti's and to school until Thursday, then I'll come back to Mum's while Mutti will be going to her place to look after my little sister. So Thursday arrives and after the end of school, I jump on a bus home to my mum's. I get there quite late in the evening. It's February, freezing cold, the snow is falling thick, and so the bus I originally got on broke down half way through. I have to wait for another bus to arrive by which time there were so many people waiting at the bus stop that when we finally climbed on the bus we were all squashed against each other like sardines.

Friday morning arrives, my mum prepares me my breakfast – some toast, an egg and a cup of milky coffee. She seems to be tiptoeing around me, in the kitchen and there is an uncomfortable silence, which in the end I decide to turn into a time of quiet contemplation. I am calm. Deadly calm. And I am determined to keep it that way. I am only but a child. There is nothing that I would be able to help them with anyway. Truth is, I know very little about my father and even less about his work and professional life. And my mum will be there with me all the way, which is reassuring.

The clock in the living room chimes 8 o'clock, mum looks out of the window and says, "The taxi is here. Time to get going."

Calm. Still calm. We put on our coats, heavy boots, hats, scarves and gloves and lock the door behind us. Outside is freezing cold and it's obvious that the previous night had continued to snow as there is fresh snow on the ground and the trees, too. My mum doesn't want to provide the neighbours with a show, and even less with food for gossip, so we get out through the back door and walk to the bottom of the garden to meet the taxi, who is waiting for us, engine running. We both climb in at the back and mum shows the taxi driver the address on a piece of paper. He is just about to pull out but as he sees the address he slams the emergency brakes on.

"I'm not taking you there!" he says, suddenly agitated, and turns around to better peer at my mum. My mum stares at him but doesn't move nor say anything.

"I'm not taking you," the man protests. "That place has bad vibes. It's a bad place. I'm not going anywhere near it!" My mum continues looking at him, then pulls out some banknotes and shoves them in his hand without saying anything. He looks at the money which is now in his hand and he seems to relent, "I'll only take you to the bottom of the hill there, then I drop you off and I turn round. You'll have to walk from there."

"Fine," says my mum and turns her head to look out of the window.

All the calm I had been practising up to that point has faded away. My heart is beating fast and my calm has been replaced by nervousness and fear. The man slowly pulls out and starts driving. I say to myself, stay calm, regain your nerve, you've always known that you were not going on a holiday; you knew where you were going, you knew it was that bad place. Keep calm, nothing's changed. I look at my boots trying to steady my mind, to focus on something else other than the frantic thoughts going through my head. Calm. Feeling a bit calmer now. Nothing's changed. There will be nothing I will be able to help them with. They will have to let me go in no time. Slowly, my heart regains its beat and my previous calmness returns when I notice the man looking in the rear mirror at my mum. Then he starts talking.

"Ma'am, why are you going to that place? You have family there? Is that is? You're going to visit family?"

My mum doesn't engage with him, instead she's still looking blankly out of the window, probably in the hope that he would stop talking to her. But he doesn't get the gist and carries on, "I've heard stories about that place…people sometimes go there and then they never come back alive, they come out dead."

At hearing this my mum violently turns her head to meet his eyes in the rear view mirror and hisses,

"That's enough! I'm not paying you for a running commentary. I'm paying you to drive us!" and that being said, she turns her head around again to stare out of the window.

A few more seconds of silence pass before the man says apologetically, "I'm sorry, ma'am, I meant no disrespect…"

By now, all idea and intention I had of staying calm had all but just jumped out of the window. I can feel my heart pounding with such force in my chest that I find it difficult to breathe. I look out of the window, desperately trying to find something to focus on so that I don't cry. I see that the snow had started to fall again and for a second I think how pretty it looks. How it's such a shame that I feel so terrified that I'm not even able to enjoy the moment. I promise myself that I will allow myself to take in the beauty of snowfall when I get back from this place we are going to, later on in the day. Then all of a sudden, I remember again what the taxi driver had just said about the place and I'm gripped by fear, thinking that I might not come back out ever again. I try really hard not to cry because I don't want to upset or let down my mum, who I know, expects me to stay strong, but I just can't help it. The tears start falling down my face and all of a sudden I feel like screaming at the top of my lungs, "I can't do this! I don't want to do this! I beg you, mum, with every cell of my body, please, please, don't let me do this! I am so, so scared!"

I turn my head to face my mum and mouth to her, "I can't do this, please don't make me…" but she just looks at me, blank expression on her face and simply whispers back, "No choice," before turning her head round to look out of the window again.

And in that moment I hate my mum for what I see to be her forcing me into a situation that had nothing to do with me, but more than that, I hate her for not offering me, in this moment of absolute desperation, of absolute desolation, the slightest comfort or reassurance. No gesture of kindness, of compassion.

And that one moment came to become the defining moment of our relationship for possibly the rest of her life, for I resented her for it and failed to understand her motivation, nor forgive her for many years to come. From that point on, I no longer allowed her the opportunity to offer me any kind of nurturing, kindness or compassion. Maybe I even no longer allowed her to be a mother to me, pretty much completely detaching myself emotionally from her for good. Eventually, after much soul searching I came to forgive her and forgive myself, too, because that day, back in that cab, I was blinded by my own fear and I failed to realise that maybe my mum was probably frozen by the same fear, too. That perhaps she was just trying to keep it together for my sake, thinking that by appearing tough, some of that toughness might rub off on me too and so, my resolution to stay strong would not falter.

Bah! By the time the taxi pulls up at the bottom of the hill as previously agreed, it is too late for any resolution to have stayed with me. I am literally trembling, filled with dread and fear. My mum pays the taxi driver the remaining amount, he jumps out of the car to open the door for my mum and myself and starts to give us directions to the place. "It's just up the hill, here on the left," but my mum cuts him short.

"I know where it is."

"Well, good luck, then," the taxi driver says and then, for whatever reason, he goes to give my mum a kiss on the cheek. My mum recoils, so taken aback and outraged by what she obviously perceives to be a completely inappropriate, over-familiar gesture, that I fear she might give him a slap. But in the end she regains her control, possibly realising that once again he meant no disrespect and that probably in his own, simple way, he was trying to show her some kind of compassion. In any case, the situation makes me giggle to myself and for just one second I forget why we are there.

We start the walk up the hill, and we hear the taxi turning back behind us, like the driver said he would. The walk up the hill is treacherous as the hill is steep and there are patches of black ice everywhere on the pavement. My mum and I are slipping and sliding all over the place, we cling onto each other to avoid a fall, grabbing at trees, the fence and finally the gate in front of the actual building.

'Calea Rahovei, Number 36 – the State Security Directorate of Penal Research'. A large, grey building with bars in front of the ground floor windows looms threateningly behind the gate.

There is a small doorway to the side of the gate with a soldier guarding it. My mum pulls out the piece of paper, the summons, and gives it to the soldier. He looks at me shyly – he is barely maybe a few years older than me – and says to my mum, "The girl will not be allowed inside."

My mum looks at him and says, "The summons is for the girl."

His eyes open wide, he looks at the summons again, then at me, mouth open in surprise and goes inside the building, asking us to wait for a second. A few seconds later, he comes back out with another young soldier in tow and we are asked to follow them both inside. My mum opens her mouth, about to say something, probably that she doesn't need to be shown the way, but thinks better of it.

We follow them inside a narrow, dark, derelict hallway with paint peeling off the walls and a few chairs along one side of the wall. One of the soldiers says, "Please. Wait here a minute," and disappears through one of the doors off the hallway. I look at the chairs next to us, but neither my mum nor I sit down. My palms are sweaty, my heart is racing, my throat feels tight, and I can barely swallow. Now that we are actually here, anticipating going into one of the rooms with the door off this hallway, I am yet again filled with fear and trepidation.

I look over at my mum who, back straight, head up, hands in her coat pocket, has her eyes fixed on the door that the young soldier had just gone inside of.

A few moments pass and the door opens. The young soldier comes out and simply says, "You can go in, now, miss," leaving the door half open and showing the way in with his hand. Both my mum and I start walking towards it, with my mum leading the way. Just before we get to the door, he steps awkwardly in front of my mum and apologetically whispers, "Ma'am, you're not allowed inside. Just the girl. You will have to wait here, please." He says to her pleadingly.

My mum stops in her tracks, is about to open her mouth in protest but in the end she just gives out a sigh. I guess she realises it's pointless.

She turns to look at me and says, "I'll be just out here, sat on one of these chairs, there."

We look at each other in silence for a second, I nod and then I cross the threshold and walk into the room in front of me.

As I walk in, at first glance, the room looks like an average, large office room, with two large desks at a perpendicular angle almost against the walls in front and to the right. On the far wall there are two large windows, both open, which I find odd given the freezing temperatures outside and how cold it is inside, too. I notice the bars on the windows and realise that I must have seen these very windows on our walk up the hill, a few minutes earlier. On the wall above the other desk, looms a large picture of Ceausescu whose seemingly benevolent, fatherly face smiles down on the room.

There are piles of paper everywhere on these desks, large manila envelopes, packets of cigarettes, lighters and also a small radio on top of the piles of paper of one of the desks. Behind the desks, there are three men; two stood up and one sat down on a chair. They all look at me intently as if inspecting me, with bemused looks on their faces, while I am stood there in front of them. I look back at them all, taking in their pale complexions with dark circles under their eyes, their cheap, polyester suits and ties, and the scratches on the dirty shoes of the two men standing up… I recognise one of them as being one of the men who had rummaged through our house all those months ago, immediately after my father's defection. Another one, I vaguely recognise as someone who had at one time, worked with my father, and who had come to our house with his wife for dinner on one occasion.

I don't know why or how but my earlier feelings of fear and trepidation have now vanished to be replaced by a slight annoyance and irritation at having to be here in this depressing place with these drab men, rather than at school with my friends.

I look around further, and I notice a smaller desk just by my left, close to the door, almost, but not quite, flush with the wall. There is a wooden chair behind it and a piece of lined paper with a pen next to it, on top of the desk. Is this desk and chair for me? I guess as much to myself and in doing so, I decide to walk round the desk, pull out the chair which is half tucked in, facing the wall and the front door. I grab the chair and half turn it around as to be able to face outward, and then I sit myself down. Thus, I am sat, with two of the men fully visible to me and one only partially.

I am still looking at them and watch how their facial expressions are noticeably changing. The bemused smiles are now replaced by frowns, flaring nostrils and serious, almost alarmed looks cast among themselves. *Mmm, pissed them off there a bit by taking it upon myself to sit down without an invite,* I think to myself, alas it's too late to change it, nor would I wish to.

"Get up right now!" hisses one of the men.

I turn my head to look at him, straight in the eye, conclude to myself that I won't respond to being spoken to worse than to a dog, so I decide to stay put.

"Get up! Nobody has given you permission to sit down!" hisses another one. I look him straight in the eye, too, but I don't move. *I refuse to respond to or engage in such rudeness,* I think to myself.

The three men exchange glances, as if to say, *Didn't quite expect this! What are we supposed to do now?* A few seconds of silence fall, before the third man, says, "State your name and date of birth."

I put my hands in my pockets and pull out my birth certificate which I was requested to bring along in compliance with the summons. I open it, stand up, and walk over to the desk where the man who asked me for my name and date of birth is sat, and I place my birth certificate in front of him. I then walk back to the chair and sit myself down again.

"State your address, citizen Baleanu," says the man who spoke first. I name my mother's address as my address as I turn my chair around a bit more to face him better. As I do so, the man who was sat down, gets up, lights up a cigarette and leaves the room. I follow him from the corner of my eye and I notice as he opens the door, that there is an armed soldier standing guard outside. *Is it to prevent my mum from walking in or me from running out?* I ask myself.

Now, one of the two men left inside the room walks over to one of their two desks and starts turning the radio knob, trying to switch it on.

"Mind if I put the radio on?" he asks. I look at him impartially without answering, knowing full well that my opinion is not really required. I faintly hear my mum's voice outside, in the corridor, though I can't make out what she's saying.

"Now, what shall we listen to? I hear you like to listen to Radio Free Europe, citizen Baleanu!" he says as he plays frantically with the frequency.

Oh, I think I know where this one is going, I think to myself. I'm still looking at him, blank expression on my face. Not betraying any thoughts or feelings.

"Is it true, Diana," asks the other man, a faint sly smile on his face, which I figure is his idea of coming across as amicable, "that you like listening to Radio Free Europe at home?"

I look at him and I find his smirk so annoying I can't resist answering him, despite better judgment.

"No, I don't like listening to the radio. The radio is for old people. I like listening to tapes, to pop music."

"Oh, tapes," the other picks up the conversation, raising his eyebrows. "And who would buy you these tapes for you?"

"I bought them, back in London, with my pocket money," I tell them.

"Oh, pocket money... Who from?" he asks.

"My mum would give it to me for babysitting my sister," I answer truthfully.

"Yes, money from the state's pocket!" the man retorts. "Well, hasn't the party and our great communist state been so generous to you over the years?" he asks. I stare at him blankly and remain quiet as I don't quite know how to answer that one.

And then the other man, the one who has now stopped fiddling with the radio dial, looks up at me and asks, "What about your grandma and your mum, don't they listen to Radio

Free Europe or Voice of America? Your grandma's old, you said old people listen to the radio…"

I turn to face him and say in my most innocent like voice, "What is Radio Free Europe? And Voice of America?"

He stares at me silently for a second, and then turns to switch back on the radio, furiously turning the dial and just like on cue – or perhaps on a tape? – the Voice of America theme song starts blasting out. I recognise it straight away but do my outmost to look indifferent and especially not to start tapping along to it. I try my hardest to look at him bored, as if I'd never heard the song before and as if it's not to my liking anyway. Eventually he switches it off and stares at me as if awaiting a reaction or a comment. I, in return, shake my head dismissively and simply say, "Never heard that song before!"

Silence. The other man, now seated, starts playing with some papers on his desk, picks one up, gets up from behind his desk and walks over to me. He places the piece of paper on the desk in front of me. He points his index finger and says, "There. Read it."

I turn around in my chair to look at this paper on the desk, and start reading the typed up paragraphs in front of me. But, even before I finish reading the heading of, "Personal declaration," I notice the name and signature at the bottom of the page. I recognise the name as that of an old friend of mine from my previous school, by mum's house. I scan read the declaration whereby she testifies that I had bragged at school of having listened to BBC World Service , Radio Free Europe and Voice of America together with my grandma and I had been encouraging her and other school friends to do the same, none of which was, of course, true. I also manage to quickly read where she mentions my constant dissatisfaction with the lack of pop culture in Romania and my frustration at not being able to openly express opinion on any matter, including the governance of the nation. I can't help thinking as I am reading all this, that somehow this is so eloquently put, using ever such grown up, sophisticated words and expressions. "The governance of the nation?" *Wow,* I think, *how did she come up with that? I'm not even quite sure what that means...would my friend have the wits to know it?*

Nevertheless, there it is, written in black and white under her name and signature... There are mentions of me, my grandma but not, interestingly, my mum. And in truth, I had never seen my mum ever actively listening to any of those radio stations. Yes, she would be in the room when my dad would switch it on, or my maternal grandma or my granddad before he had passed away, but my mum? Never! She would never be the one switching on the radio, searching for the crackling sound of one of those stations... When I would listen to it, I would do it in my bedroom, so that I could listen to the sound of the latest pop songs, to daydream a little about the life I enjoyed in London with my school friends back there, to loose myself in the memories.

Hmm...music. Such a powerful means to evoke a millions thoughts and feelings and dreams. I would also listen to those stations, a bit like my mum had, when someone in the house would switch it on to listen to the latest uncensored headlines and news about our country and region – if you can call the former communist bloc a region. Not that I would truly or fully understand a lot of what was being said, but enough to realise that there were a whole lot of people, both on the inside of the country and the outside of it, increasingly discontent with and disconnected from the politics of the land, of the region, and a way of life imposed upon no longer willing citizens. I remember having heard on Radio Free Europe about Brasov and the locals' uprising against the government as well as its devastating aftermath of deaths, injuries and arrests at the hands of Ceausescu's henchmen. And how not even that brutal repression would act any longer as a deterrent to other cities which continued to show their discontent at an increasing rate, Bucharest included.

And living in Bucharest, it was something even I would come across on occasion. Subtle signs of tacit protest against the current status quo of the country, verbal messages passed on in the street, strangers asking passers-by to quietly take a stand against the totalitarian powers of the country by switching off the lights at home at a given time of a particular evening or by quietly and unassumingly turning up at a particular public meeting place and simply stand there together as a large group, without uttering a word. Or being asked to simply refuse to stop in our tracks and stand still, as required to do when Ceausescu's daily cavalry of police and secret service cars would accompany him at high speed going to and from his offices. Instead, we would be urged to just quietly go about our daily business, indifferent to the fuss, as a sign of protest.

"So, what do you have to say now?" one of the men in the room who is stood by the radio asks me, bringing me back from my previous reverie. "Not so brazen now, are we?"

I look again at the piece of paper in front of me, shrug my shoulders and pull a face as if to dismiss the gravity of the words upon the page.

"All lies. Nothing but lies." I say and just as I'm about to turn round and face them again, the man stood closest to me leaps up and slaps me hard across the face.

"Lies?" he bellows. "You dare to call these lies?" he asks again, pointing to the paper. "This girl's esteemed father has been in the loyal service of our country's security service all of his life! And you, a traitor's daughter, dare to ascertain her words as lies?"

I look at him but barely make sense of what he is saying as his slap not only hit my cheek but also managed to hit the side of my ear, which is now ringing violently. I notice how after his lips finish moving, he stops and stares at me as if expecting an answer. I know that it's my turn to say something but I can't even open my mouth, I can't think, can't pretty much focus on anything. My left year is ringing so violently I feel so dizzy, like I'm about to pass out. I put my head down on my arms, on the desk, just for a second, I think to myself, until I get to steady myself a little.

As I do so, with my eyes half open, I notice the man who had just slapped me, casually lighting up a cigarette and walking out of the room. The moment he walks out, I hear the other man, the one who is still in the room with me, asking me something about my life back in London. My thoughts drift to that time, which seems so long ago now, like a distant dream, a life which now seems as far away as it seems unreal. Still, the ringing in my ear lessens a little and with my head still down on my arms, as it feels too heavy to lift, I mumble something about having been to school in London. The man wanders over to where I am sat, kicks my chair and asks me to sit up straight when I address him. It takes all of my willpower and strength to prop my head up with my hands. I try to add something else about my recollection of London, perhaps something about my after school activities, my tennis or swimming sessions, but I reconsider, so I keep my mouth shut.

The man who had walked out a few minutes earlier, now walks back in, and he's looking particularly hyped up. He comes right up next to me and stands hovering over me. Straight away he starts firing question after question, barely pausing in between to allow me to answer.

"Who were the people your parents would socialise with in London? Was there a particular man they would meet frequently? What was his name? Was it that Adam Reid? Answer the goddamn questions!"

I try to keep up with the questions fired at me and shake my head at every question, which is all I can muster to do. "Your mother says she doesn't understand much English but we have it on good authority that you're fluent in English. You could understand everything that was said. So, tell us! What was discussed? What would your father talk about with this man?"

I want to tell him that I have no idea what he's talking about, that I would hardly spend any time with my father in London and on the very rare occasions I'd go to an evening reception with my parents, there would be so many people, I never truly registered any of their names, even less what would be said or discussed.

"Answer my questions!" he shouts menacingly, having completely lost control. "What would they be talking about?" I look at him blankly, the ringing in my ear now quite faint, but I find his aggression too intimidating and so I refuse to interact with him. He looks back at me, naked anger written all over his face, heavily breathing through his flaring nostrils. And then, just like so, he grabs me by the upper arm and punches me in the back.

I jump up and enraged, I scream, "Get off me!" as I instinctively push him off. He is a tall, slim man and I don't know whether it's the angle that I find myself at or perhaps because he is not expecting it, but as I clumsily push him off, he loses his balance and half collapses on one of the desks behind him. He looks outraged by what had just happened and for one second I literally fear for my life at the thought of what might happen next. A few seconds pass with him standing still, breathing heavily and staring menacingly at me and then slowly, he seems to be regaining some of his composure.

He straightens up and storms out of the door but not before saying, "Oh, how you'll pay for this," to me, over his shoulder.

I am now alone with the other man who had acted as a mere spectator to the preceding events. He has now lit up a cigarette which he is smoking, sat down, behind his desk. He looks at me through the thick, bluish smoke, a look filled with disgust mixed with disbelief. Then, he casually says, "There is a piece of paper and a pen right there on that little desk, by your side. It's Friday, we all want to go home early, so c'mon let's put this story to bed. I'll tell you what to write, just be a good girl, pick up the pen and write down as I tell you."

I twist round in my chair to look at the paper and think that I feel so sickened and dejected by everything that's happened this morning so far, I no longer care if I go home or not, or even if I ever get out of that room or not.

"C'mon, let's start with 'I, the undersigned, by the name of Baleanu Ioana Diana, domiciled…wherever it is you said that you live…'" he says with a wave of a hand.

I pick up the pen and start writing, thinking to myself that so far it's fine, all true, nothing controversial. He sees me writing and I catch a glimpse of him as I half turn waiting for the next instalment. Self-satisfied smile on his face, he says,

"Good! See how well we get on!" and with a nod of the head, is encouraging me to carry on.

"'I hereby testify that I have frequently and in the company of my mother, Baleanu Eugenia, listened to the Radio stations Voice of America and Radio Free Europe.'"

I finish writing, put my pen down and turn around to face him. He realises that I had finished writing far too early to have included everything he mentioned, and his seemingly benevolent smile turns into a cold stare. We look at each other for what seems minutes, though in reality, it's probably mere seconds, while he considers his next move. Then, he suddenly pushes his chair back, walks round his desk and comes to pick up the piece of paper off the desk. Standing by my side, he reads silently for a few seconds, puts the paper back down on the table and walks out of the room, slamming the door shut behind him.

I realise that it's the first time today that I find myself alone in this room and I take a deep breath. I look around the room and notice the clock on the wall. 10.30 am. I've already been here for two hours. Just as I'm starting to wonder what will happen next, if I will finally be allowed to go home, I overhear a cacophony of arguing voices outside, a few male ones and one female – my mother's.

The door then opens with a thud and my mother walks right in, right past me. I can tell that she's noticed me out of the corner of her eye, but she is barely looking at me. She strolls right in, chin a little higher than most people, with the confidence of a general, as if she was daring anyone to cross her. Hell! As if she was the actual person in charge of this place, as if she owned the place, knowing it inside out and expecting her word to be law. My mum's utmost unfaltering confidence regardless of the situation is something which would never cease to awe me throughout my life, and no more so than in that very moment.

"Popescu, Radulescu, that's enough!" she says, as if giving an order to the men trawling behind her, which in comparison, now look as if they're following like two obedient dogs at their owner's feet.

"Time for her to politely say goodbye and for me to take her home!" she bellows turning to stare at them, index finger pointing at them, angry expression on her face. She comes across as intimidating even to me and her anger is not even directed at me.

"I've done as expected," she carries on, "I respected your request. You can tick that off your list, but that's it, now! Enough! Time to go home, she's got nothing to say."

The men look at her and shake their heads. One of them, the one she referred to as Radulescu, speaks first, "Gina, you're a pain, you're obstinate, we get it…"

"But," the other one, the one my mum referred to as Popescu picks up the thread, "this one is just a tough little nut to crack. She just needs a little persuasion. And who better to do it than her own mother?" he finishes with a smirk.

"Go on," continues Radulescu, "tell her to talk to us, to tell us about who listens to Radio Free Europe and Voice of America in the family. What would Vergil spend hours talking about with all those men he would meet, without permission, when posted in London…"

My mum looks at them and sighs like she is bored, walks over to where the radiator is and where Popescu is now sitting with his back against it and says to him, "Move!" He moves away without questioning it and my mum takes his place, sitting with her back against the radiator, presumably to warm up.

And for the first time since walking into this office, she turns to face me and looks me in the eye. Her stare is blank, impartial as is mine in return. I see her putting on a fake smile and then saying in a sweet voice which I don't recognise as one ever being used by her, "Diana, my darling girl, can you please tell these men what it is that you know about family members listening to Radio Free Europe or Voice of America? And any men that you know your father might have met with, when in London?"

The men look at each other, sighing heavily, shaking their heads, clearly obvious of my mother's sarcasm and therefore disappointed in her actions. I am looking from my mum to the men in the room, shrugging my shoulders, but not actually saying anything.

Then, unexpectedly and with a loud bang, the door flies open and what looks to be a mountain of a man, engulfed in cigarettes smoke from his lit Kent cigarette, which is shaking between his fingers, thunderously storms in.

As he does so, the two men in the room jump up and stand stiff as if to attention. My mum watches him, bored expression on her face, though I notice straight away the tiniest, subtlest ripple of some emotion that resembles fear, in her eyes. The man looks crazed with rage, breathing heavily and looking wildly around the room. The hand with which he is holding the cigarette is shaking so violently I wonder if he might not be a Parkinson's sufferer. But then I notice his fast-paced and assured strides and doubt if Parkinson's might be the reason.

He leaps towards my mother, picking up a chair which is in his way and literally flings it across the room. He stops in front of her, puts the cigarette in his mouth and goes to punch my mum square in the face. My mum, as if anticipating it, ducks out of his punch way, he misses, she straightens up slightly and while she does so, she punches him in the face instead. It's all happening in silence, as if it's a well-rehearsed dance, which makes me wonder how many times a scene such as this must have played out between the two of them, when my mother had been brought here to be interrogated herself.

Following the punch received, the man doesn't miss a step, my mother's punch not so much as having slowed him down. He grabs my mother by the throat and bangs her head against the wall behind her.

"Tell her to write what the fuck we tell her to, to fucking sign it and then both of you can get the fuck out of my place!" he tells her, her throat still in his clutch.

My mum is staring in his eyes, breathing shallowly, desperately scratching at his hand, the one around her neck. I know if she could, she would be saying plenty, but the man's hand round her throat is preventing her from opening her mouth. He holds his grip for a few more seconds which feel like hours.

I am overwhelmed by panic, anxiously asking myself if I should not do something; jump on his back, or hit him over the head with something – but what? – to force him to let go of my mum. However, it's as if I'm frozen to the spot in fear and in bewilderment at what is happening.

Eventually, he lets go of her throat and bellows, "Get her out of here!" pointing at my mum, but without looking at anyone in particular. "You two get out of here, too!" and this time he nods his head at the two men present.

Both Popescu and Radulescu go over to where my mum is and try to grab her by the arms in order to walk her out. She slaps their hands away, shouting, "Hands off me, you peasants!" not beaten down for one nanosecond by the previous encounter with the man, whom I later find out is Colonel Gheorghe Vasile, head of the Calea Rahovei unit, Department of Romania's state security penal investigations.

And as she walks out of the room, my mum is still shouting at the top of her lungs, "As for you, Vasile, you are nothing but a degenerate, illiterate imbecile, your brain so limited in intellect you can't even fight with words, all you know to do is use your fists like the goddamn criminal that you are!"

The door shuts behind her, but I can still hear her ranting and shouting insults beyond it. Eventually, a few seconds of silence fall as the man waits, as if to hear the end of my mum's monologue.

Yet again, I naively think that the man my mum had referred to as Vasile would now let me go, too. And so, nothing prepares me for what follows instead. For Vasile looks at me, lets out an animal like grunt and leaps forward, unleashing a torrent of punches on my back, the back of my head and top of my arms. I feel pain like I had never felt it before in my life, like my whole body is about to split open. I try to shelter my head with my hands from the rain of blows but to no avail. Mixed with the physical pain, but more acutely so, I feel raw rage and anger at the meaningless and mindless injustice of it all. I want to stand up and return some of his punches or at least fight him off somehow, but the speed of his blows is relentless and as I am sat down, I cannot find an opportunity to move from my current position. Eventually, the punches stop and the moment this happens, I somehow find the strength to jump up to my feet to face this beast now stood in front of me. I want him to see the anger mixed with defiance on my face, for I don't want him to believe for one second that I will get cowered by the violence with which he is so obviously trying to break me.

He is red in the face and breathing heavily, seemingly tired by the effort undertook in administering the beating. "Write and sign the fucking testimony," he says to me between breaths, now almost nose to nose with me.

I look him in the eyes and simply yet loudly and clearly say, "No."

"No?" he screams back. "No fucker says no to me, you shit! Do you realise who I am?" he shouts, spit flying out of his mouth.

I am under no doubt by the way he behaves and by my mum's reaction as well as that of Popescu and Radulescu when Gheorghe Vasile first walked into the office, that he is the one in charge around here.

Still, I look at him right in the eye and perhaps emboldened by my mum's earlier behaviour towards him, perhaps remembering my great-grandma's words of advice about not being cowered, but mainly because I am just raging inside at the cruel injustice of the situation, I answer back to him with, "I don't give a shit about who you are! I am not writing or signing your lies!"

He stares at me incredulously, eyes about to pop out of their sockets, then he unpredictably spins round, fixes his sight on one of the two desks and with one leap forward, he pulls the top drawer of the desk closest to the radiator open and grabs out a gun.

He's got the gun in his hand, he flicks open the cylinder and looks at the chamber. Satisfied at what he sees, he closes the cylinder and walks over to me. I look at him still feeling little else other than rage. I can't explain why, but fear is not an emotion I'm experiencing right now. My mind is telling me that I should, but I don't. It's as if I'm having an out of body experience whereby I'm not just the participant but also the spectator in this never ending drama.

Gun pointed in my direction he walks right over to me and what I notice more so than the gun itself, is the fact that his hand is shaking so violently I can't help thinking that he might actually drop the gun. I also see the drops of sweat that have formed on this man's forehead and how his chest is heaving with every breath he takes.

He comes up to me, grabs me by the face with one hand and with the other he points the gun at the top of my forehead. He tells me, staring me in the eyes, "You will write and sign that fucking piece of paper. Or else I will pull this trigger. Do you understand me, you shit? Nod to show me you understand."

I look right back at him and I know that I will not sign that piece of paper. No way. Not now. Not after all I'd gone through this day so far. Not after having come face to face with this monster. I don't know why I feel so strongly. Stubbornness? Perhaps. Is it because I'd had enough of the charade that had been playing out all day? Maybe. Or is it a young person's feeling of immortality? Not really. For I was pretty convinced that my life was about to end shortly. So I guess I just wanted to take back some control over the way I thought my life was going to end that day. I was not prepared to allow this monster to be the one determining my ultimate fate, to be the one ending my life. And so, as he is looking at me in the eyes and me right back at him, I somehow raise my hand, put it over his, the one holding the gun and I quickly squeeze the trigger. I close my eyes and expect to meet my end. Calmly and on my own terms.

The gun makes a faint sound, more like a short, half-hearted cough but then nothing. Except for a bit of a dull pain at the top of my forehead, where the barrel had been pointing.

Gheorghe Vasile, visibly taken aback now, allows his mouth to drop slightly open, involuntarily. He stares at me for one more second then he throws the gun down onto one of the desks.

What happened? I ask myself. A question I will continue to ask, I guess, for the rest of my life, since to this day I cannot give myself a feasible explanation. Was there no bullet in the chamber? Did the bullet get stuck? Did I not squeeze the trigger sufficiently? Truth is, I guess, I will never know what actually happened. But I would like to think that maybe some divine intervention was at work that very moment…

In any case, Gheorghe Vasile quickly regains his wits and his viciousness is back in full force.

"I'll have every single soldier guarding this place rape your fucking brains out until you decide to sign this paper," he threatens me and he storms out of the door.

A few minutes pass and the enormity of what had just happened compounded by what he had just said start to dawn on me. I begin to shake uncontrollably and I am now desperately trying to think of finding a way out of this place. I look at the windows but I know already that they have thick bars in front of them with no large enough gaps between them to make escaping a possibility. There are no other doors, except for the one that Gheorghe Vasile had just stormed out of and I know that that door is guarded by an armed soldier on the other side. Every time someone had come in or gone out of this door, I could notice the armed guard, rifle over his shoulder, standing to attention just outside the door.

In the end, I sit down at my desk and just as I'm about to resign myself to my fate, and put my head down on the desk in despair, the door opens. Two animated women, both smoking, walk straight in. They seem in a hurry.

"C'mon, follow us," one of them says to me with a wave of hand.

I look at the time, which will be, even though I don't know it at the time, the last time I would be able to do so in a long while. The clock says 11.27 am. I stand up and follow them out, still shaking uncontrollably, my teeth clattering in my mouth with shock but also now feeling the freezing cold.

I keep following them as they walk out of the office, down the dark, derelict corridor where I desperately look around for my mum, expecting to see her waiting on one of the chairs which were lining the corridor there when we first arrived but which are now all gone, my mum included. I feel so alone, so abandoned and for the first time today, real animal like fear takes over completely, constantly expecting the unexpected to happen again.

A door opens and we walk into a huge, bare room but just for three chairs by one of the three huge, curtainless bay windows and a steel framed, hospital type bed, against one of the walls. There is also a small steel table at the side of the bed.

One of the women points to the steel framed bed and says, "Right, take your jeans and your pants off and lie down on that bed, there!"

I look at the dirty, stained mattress of the bed, which has no sheet nor cover, and I cross my arms to steady my shaking, but I make no attempt to lie down.

One of the women comes over to where I am stood, not far from the door and pulls me along by my coat. I then start crying, sobbing and more than anything, shaking so badly, I'm afraid my legs will buckle under me. I softly whisper to her, through my sobs, "Please, I beg of you, don't," but she ignores me, pulls me along, pushes me down on the mattress and they both start taking my boots and jeans off. I'm desperately protesting, sobbing, and weakly trying to kick them off as I notice the door opening and a number of soldiers filing in and lining up just by the door.

I'm still trying to fight off the women who are now taking off my jeans and whom I suspect are getting me ready to be raped by the soldiers who had just entered the room, just as Gheorghe Vasile had threatened earlier, before he had disappeared. I carry on pleading with these two women and through my tears I take in the fact that these soldiers, all young boys, probably of 17 or 18 years of age, are looking at me furtively and then averting their gaze in embarrassment, shuffling their feet, looking at the floor uncomfortably, as if they themselves don't actually want to be there, in that situation, possibly any more than I do.

"Please, don't let it happen!" I'm still begging the women whilst sobbing and shaking like a leaf, now both my trousers and pants having been taken off. One of the women, turns around to where the small table is, fiddles with something for a moment. When she turns around, surgical gloves now on, she forces my legs open with the help of the other woman, pokes her fingers into my vagina, and then brings her fingers up in front of her eyes. She peers at her fingers and then walks off, casually saying to me, over her shoulder, "You can get dressed now."

At first, I feel as though I misunderstood what she had said but I see the other woman walking away now and losing interest in me too. Still sobbing, I quickly grab my clothes and try to start getting dressed. At the same time, I see the woman who had poked me in the vagina taking her gloves off and with a nod of the head, gesturing to the soldiers to get out.

"What's up?" the other woman now asks her.

"She's still a virgin," I hear the other one replying, shrugging.

"Hmm. He's not going to be happy when he hears it. I'm not telling him!" says the other woman quietly but resolutely.

"And then what?" snaps the first woman, now disposing of the surgical gloves in a small paper bag. "You're going to allow a girl who's still a virgin to be raped instead?" she hisses back. "That's what he said, after all. If she's still a virgin, to let her off. We're only doing as instructed. C'mon, off you go to let him know!" she orders the other woman, who hesitantly starts walking towards the door.

Meanwhile I'm trying my hardest to get dressed but my hands and my whole body is still shaking so violently I can't even manage to put my jeans on. The woman looks over to where I am and sees me struggling. She walks over to me, and helps me put on my jeans.

"You've gone into shock," she says matter of factly, barely looking at me, concentrating on my jeans instead. "You need some quiet time for a while. And some water. I'll try to get that for you."

My clothes are finally all back on, though I still can't stop myself from sobbing and shaking. I am starting to feel a little warmer and that is somewhat comforting. The woman walks out of the room and here I am all alone. Still very frightened by the experience which I had just had, but also because I don't know what terrorising and agonising situation might follow next. Just like a wounded animal, I instinctively find a corner, where I sit down on the hard, cold floor, hugging my knees, as if trying to hide from view, though at the same time, knowing full well how exposed I must be. The shaking starts to subdue a little as I warm up slightly, but I still can't stop myself from crying.

I hear the two women's voices before I see them walking back into the room, at the same time. One of them has a glass of water which she offers me and I drink thankfully.

"Why don't you just sign the testimony? That way you can just go home," she asks as if pleading with me whilst I'm drinking the water.

Why don't I sign the testimony? I ask myself. You might wonder, too. But I know full well why I hadn't sign it and why I am never going to, either. For, you see, I don't care what happens to me. Despite the fear I'm feeling, I still don't care if I live or die, though in that moment I would truthfully prefer death, of the quick kind. But, I do care what happens to my mum and implicitly to my sister. I don't want my little sister growing up without a mother. Having had a sister, in time, she would probably forget, I tell myself. But you can't forget having had a mother. She'd spend her whole life wondering, searching, asking questions. And how could I ever be able to look her in the eye knowing that I would have been the cause of her growing up without a mother, that I would have been to blame for her mother's imprisonment, maybe even her death.

I shake my head and between sobs I say, "I'm not signing. I can't do it…"

The women look at each other, raise their shoulders as if to say, *What else is there left for us to do?* Then one of them says to me, "C'mon! Get up and follow us."

I stand up, not even considering arguing with them, despite the dread at what might follow next. I follow them out of the room, down the derelict corridor, down a spiral staircase and then another narrow, dark, damp and smelly corridor. Along the corridor, on the right side, we walk past a number of steel doors. I have never been to a prison before but somehow I know straight away that these steel doors must lead inside prison cells. Calm. At once, I feel surreally calm and detached. No more tears. Just calm.

The women stop in front of one such door, and I stop right behind them. One of them gets a bunch of keys out of her coat pocket, unlocks and opens the door. She turns towards me and asks me to take my boots' laces off and hand her my scarf. "This is going to be where you will get your quiet time for a while. And thinking time. Until you decide that you're ready to sign the testimony."

I do as asked, take my boots' laces off and my scarf and hand them to her. She makes a gesture with her hand as if showing me the way in, though neither of them seems keen on going inside to show me around.

"Can I please see my mum before I go in?" I plead. They both look at me visibly annoyed by my request.

"You're mum's gone home. Quite a long time ago now."

It seems strange to me that my mum would have gone home given that she said before we had got here that she would wait for me no matter what.

I silently enter the cell. I expected a dingy, stark room but nothing could have prepared me for the sight of it. A small, damp room with the cement broken on the floor and the paint on the walls long since peeled off but replaced instead by disgusting filth. No windows, just a long neon light flickering above, on the ceiling. A steel frame bed with a filthy mattress not dissimilar to the one I had experienced in the room upstairs. A bucket in a corner which once might have been white but which now stood caked in dirt and possibly blood. This was going to be my new place of solitude. For how long? I didn't dare wonder. Or ask.

"You go to the toilet in the bucket," I hear one of the two women saying from the other side of the threshold, still unwilling to venture in. "And someone will bring you some food and water in a while."

And with that being said, the door closes right in front of me. I hear the key turning in the lock and the sound of their footsteps fading away.

Is this really happening to me? I ask myself. *Or is it just a horrifying nightmare from which I will shortly wake up?*

I feel drained and tired all of a sudden and consider where I might be able to rest my body for a while. The mattress looks so disgusting that I can't bring myself to sit on it. I find a corner of the room which, even though is dirty and damp, it's a far sight better than the mattress. The sound of the flickering neon light above me acts like an annoying wasp buzzing around, which I find impossible to ignore and of course since there is no visible switch, I can't turn off. Eventually though, tiredness must have got the better of me. At some point, I must have somehow slid into that nameless place between reality and sleep. When I open my eyes again, I notice that a tray of food had been left on the floor, just inside my cell by the door.

I am indeed feeling starved, for I haven't had anything to eat since breakfast, so I decide to go take a look. Alas, I should not have bothered for as soon as I get close enough to the tray, I notice not only a nondescript plate of food but more notably a fury of cockroaches devouring the bread. Disgusted, I turn away and decide to take my place back in the corner where I had drifted off previously, but I panic at the thought of the cockroaches finding their way over and crawling all over me as I might drift asleep again. Instead, I start pacing the cell whilst jumping and down at intervals to warm up, as a damp cold which I can't shake off seems to have taken hold of me. A while after I start doing so, I hear a key turning in the lock and the door slowly opening. I stop in the middle of the cell uncertain as to what to expect.

The door opens fully and an elderly man wearing a big thick kaki coat walks in, slightly limping. He sees the tray by the threshold and goes to pick it up but in doing so, he catches a glimpse of me. I don't quite know why, but when he sees me he stops what he's doing and he peers at me, visibly astonished.

"We're imprisoning children now, I see," is all I catch as he mumbles to himself. He then picks up the tray and eventually walks out, closing and then locking the door behind him.

Now that the tray is gone the cockroaches start to scatter. I am still too cold and disgusted to sit on the floor in case the cockroaches return, so I consider kicking the mattress off the bed to see if I might not be able to make for myself a place of relative rest on the steel bedframe. I'm still considering this, where and how I'd kick the mattress off, when I hear footsteps outside the door followed by the now familiar sound of the key turning in the lock.

The door opens and the elderly man who had earlier picked up the food tray, walks back in. I can see that he is carrying a thermos and a small packet covered in a plain white cloth. He sits himself down on the edge of the disgusting mattress not fazed by its filth. He holds out his hand as if offering me the small package.

"Ham and cheese sandwich," he simply says.

I am reluctant to take it and look at it and him suspiciously, not understanding his motivation. "Take it. Have it a little later if you want. My wife made it for me, for my dinner during my shift tonight. But you have it! I am sure you need it more than me…"

I take the small package from his hand and hold it, unopened, in mine for I'm not sure where to put it, whilst continuing to watch the man. Meanwhile he then turns his attention to the thermos, unscrewing the cap and then pouring a piping hot liquid into the cup of the thermos top. He extends it to me and this time I don't need much encouragement. The smell of some kind of a soup fills the cell and it's now making me feel almost delirious with hunger. I take the cup to my lips and gulp the contents down. The soup – although under different circumstances no doubt nowhere near as flavoursome as the soups my grandma would make for me –

tastes in the moment like *manna* from the heavens, the most delicious thing I have ever tried.

When I finish drinking it, I hand the cup back to the man saying a soft "Thank you". In return he nods his head, fills up the cup and hands it back to me again. I finish the second cup just as he gets up. Before taking the cup from me he mumbles something which at first makes me think that he's talking to himself. "…You hang in there because they can't hold you here for too long. You're merely a child. They'll have to let you go soon enough!" I realise that he's actually talking to me but I don't have the opportunity to reply because he's already out of the door. Before he closes it, he finishes by saying, "I'll bring you some more to eat tomorrow," and then he locks the door firmly behind him.

Once he's gone I feel exhausted again. I'm determined to kick the mattress off the bed, which after a few attempts I manage to do. I place my body on the steel frame of the bed which although uncomfortable is not as painful as the hard, damp floor. I rest my head, hat on, against the steel headrest and close my eyes. I don't know how much time passed with me sat there, like that… Minutes? Hours, more likely.

I drift in and out of sleep or better said in and out of consciousness. I sometimes dream, sometimes wonder if I would ever see my family again. *Why hasn't anyone come to get me or at least come to see me?* I ask myself over and over again. *My mum, my grandma? Where are they?* My mind drifts to thoughts of my dad and whether I would ever see him again. And I also think of the meaning of all of this. This never ending ordeal that my mum, my grandma and now myself am going through. The purpose of my father's defection. His words whilst arguing with my mum all those months ago. How he wanted to, how he was going to make a difference, a change for the people of this country. Yes, he defected but nothing had changed. His defection had brought about no change for the people. Just to our lives. And not for the better. For here I am, in a prison cell. When I should have been at home, playing with my sister, being silly and laughing with my friends, putting on makeup, listening to music, preparing my homework in time for school...

I also wonder if my father and those that he had defected to, stopped to consider for even a second the impact of their actions on his own family. Had his family's welfare even been of any concern or consequence at all, to them all? I was left wondering about this, for a long time, though I was not to know that around that very time, my father's desperation had become so intense at hearing – from the underground – about our treatment, that one day he walked straight into the Romanian embassy. He told the ambassador at the time that he was willing to hand himself in, in exchange for his family's safety. At which, the said ambassador sniggered at my father's request, incarcerated him, spent the night making several phone calls to Bucharest, before (fortunately, in retrospect, though quite puzzling given the circumstances at the time) showing my father the door, asking him to get out and not bother him with his presence ever again...

Still, given the deafening silence heard at that painful time of injustice and abuse which we endured as a family, the jubilation of those my father had defected to, at having scored one against the communist bloc, must have been the only thing that truly mattered. Their only consideration.

I must have eaten the sandwich given to me by the old guard, at some point, though I don't have any recollection of when or how. When I wake up, by the sound of another food tray being dumped on the floor of my cell by a soldier who thereafter quickly retreats, I instinctively feel inside my coat pocket for the sandwich given to me earlier by the old guard. But all I get to pull out are a few crumbs and the cloth in which the sandwich had been wrapped.

Not long after, he comes into my cell again and repeats the generosity of what I guess must now have been the previous day or night – for I can no longer make sense of time. Only that this time he pulls out a sandwich of his own and he sits on the edge of the bed, eating his own one by my side, as I drink the hot soup he offered once again.

And once I finish drinking the soup, I look at him and wonder why he is doing what he is doing. I turn to face him and ask him as much. He answers without looking at me, but staring at the floor, as if talking to the top of his boots, "Sometimes in life, miss, you are told that this is right, this is the right thing to do and this is what you should do. But when you feel it in your heart that, that is not quite the right thing to do, then you can't help but do what you think it's right."

I shed a tear quietly then, partly because I remember my mum's words when her doctor friend came to the house to assess my grandma's injuries following their first arrest. How she had said that despite all the evil in the world, the universe sometimes conspires to send you a message of goodwill and kindness in the shape of a compassionate person. But also, I shed a tear partly because here he was, this man, a stranger to me and probably not knowing much about the reasons of my incarceration, yet willing to offer me not than just a slice of food but show me the act of kindness and generosity, too. Quite possibly putting his job and perhaps even his own life at risk in doing so. I guess that's the thing about humanity – sometimes it visits in unexpected ways. And to say that I was grateful then, in that moment, is an understatement. For I will forever remember and bless this man, in my thoughts, wherever he may be.

Following the old guard's departure, I yet again drift in the now habitual pattern of in and out of consciousness. Neon light above still buzzing and flickering. Cockroaches crawling on the floor and sometimes up the walls. At other times, I'd hear a scratching sound on the other side of the door which I presume to be rats trying to get in.

At some point, I hear the cell lock turning and the door opening. I try my hardest to focus as my mind can barely distinguish between what is real and what is not, anymore. A soldier, a boy, rifle over his shoulder, walks in and stands over me.

"Miss," he says softly, awaiting a reaction. I don't respond, partly because I'm not sure if I'm dreaming or if this is actually happening.

"Miss," he says again, a bit louder and shakes my shoulder as if to wake me up. I make an effort to sit upright and face him.

"You're free to go," he says looking at me curiously, as if trying to work out if I am fully awake or not. If I can understand what he is saying or not. I feel like half smiling but it takes too much effort. I know now that I'm surely dreaming. I lie back down on the bed, close my eyes and try to lick my cracked lips for my mouth has become so dry.

"Miss. C'mon! You have to go now," he says again, this time his voice a little more urgently.

"Go where?" I must have asked him, because even though the question crossed my mind I didn't think I had said it out loud.

But I must have done for he replies, "You can go home, now." I frown and look at him bewildered as I'm starting to regain consciousness a little now. He looks at me impatiently but also with a look of pity in his eyes. I, in return measure him up and down, and ask myself if this might not be a trap of sorts. I gather that I had been summoned here, to this place, at the request of a colonel, the head of the establishment, I had been incarcerated no doubt at the request of the same colonel, and now, a young soldier has the authority to tell me that I can go home? I am sceptical and beyond puzzled.

"Who are you to tell me that I can go home now?" I ask him, possibly coming across quite rude, though that is not my intention. The words just happen come out as such.

"They asked me to do it. To tell you that you can go home now. The people upstairs," he finishes with a glance towards the ceiling.

I sit up and then slowly come off the bed. My legs feel like jelly. My whole body does. And I still don't trust a word this soldier tells me but I decide to follow him out anyway. What choice do I have? My boots have no laces and so with every step I take I trip over a little, my feet constantly coming out of my boots.

"I need my boots laces back. I can't walk properly without them. And a glass of water. Please," I tell the soldier as we start making our way up the spiral staircase, the very same one I remember going down on, with the two women, how long ago now, I ask myself, though I can't be sure. We get to the top of the stairs and I follow him onto the main corridor. The one leading from the front door of this building, where I can now see again the small row of chairs which were there when my mum and I had first arrived here.

"Sit down for a minute," the soldier says pointing towards one of the chairs. I sit down and in doing so, I catch a glimpse of my reflection in one of the windows opposite. Even though it's quite dark in this corridor, I nevertheless see my matted hair and filthy face. Embarrassed by my appearance, I frantically try to run my fingers through my hair and pull it back in a top knot, whilst rubbing my face clean with the sleeve of my coat, in order to tidy myself up a little. I stop at once though, as I suddenly hear loud, angry male voices coming from behind the door at the bottom of the corridor. The door behind which I had been interrogated myself. When? I still have no idea how long ago now it must have been. For a while, I fear that the door might open any minute now and that I would be summoned back in, going all over again the ordeal of having to refuse to sign a testimony that I don't want to admit to. I recognise some of the voices behind the door, and by the heated exchange with an unknown, defensive voice, I realise that now their anger is directed towards someone else. Whom? I don't know. A man, given the male pleading voice. Some other victim of crass injustice and cruel brutality, I imagine…

The soldier returns with a mug of water, as well as my laces and the scarf, all of which I had forgotten about. I take the mug and quickly gulp the water down. Water. Sacred water. Quenches the thirst, nourishes the soul. He hands me the laces and I start tying them to my boots. The soldier is standing next to me watching.

"So, I can really go home now?" I ask him again, incredulous.

"Yes," he answers, without adding anything else.

"Can I call my mum, to ask her to come get me?" I ask him.

"No," he answers back. "No phone calls."

"Can I borrow some money so that I can take a bus home? Or call my mum from a pay phone?" I ask, trying to figure out how I would get home without my mum, without any money. He half smiles, making me think that he believes my request to be outlandish.

"No money either," he answers.

Laces tied up, I stand up, getting my hat and gloves out of my coat pocket and put them on as well as the scarf. He starts walking towards the front door and I follow him once again. I'm still reluctant to believe that I am finally about to be released. I don't even dare to hope, in case I might be tempting fate. *Keep putting one foot in front of the other. Let's see how far you'll get,* I tell myself.

The front door opens and daylight dazzles me at once. I squint and rub my eyes and squint some more as my eyes are trying to adjust to a different form of light having been constantly exposed to the neon light of the cell for so long. How long? I ask myself yet again. But I dare not ask the soldier since I don't want to further postpone my possible departure from this place of horrors. Once we are past the threshold, the soldier takes his guarding position outside the front door and points to the gate door in front of us, "That way out. Safe journey."

I look at the gate and the soldier standing guard just outside the gate door and wonder if that might not be where my journey will end. The soldier on the gate door being the one who decides to turn me back and then it would all turn out to be nothing but a cruel joke.

Still, I walk down the steps and across the courtyard towards the gate door and take in a deep breath of fresh air. Pure, crisp, well, freezing cold air, rather. But it feels like bliss. It feels like morning air, though it could really be any time of the day. And with every breath, it's like a fresh new life force is seeping through every cell of my body. Whilst I'm still walking, there is a break in the cloud and a ray of sunshine peeks out to caress my cheek. I stop, close my eyes and smile, feeling its warmth for a few seconds.

Before long I'm standing in front of the gate door and the soldier standing guard on the other side. He hears my footsteps and turns. He looks at me and I feel like my head is spinning. My heart feels like it has stopped beating for I have stopped breathing for sure. *Will I be turned back?*

"Two steps back, please, miss," he says.

I do as I'm told but for a second my mind goes blank and I fear that I might just pass out. *Is this it? Is this as far as I will get to leaving this place?* I watch silently as the soldier reaches for the gate door handle, pushes it down and opens the door towards me. The door is now wide open and the soldier is standing to the side, making way for me to get past. I slowly and hesitantly walk past, out of the courtyard and step onto the pavement outside. Then I keep walking, not looking over my shoulder, though expecting any second now to be called back. But I am not. So I keep on walking. Back down the same hill my mum and I had climbed after the taxi dropped us off at the bottom of it. Keep walking. One foot in front of the other. Look forward. Don't look back. There is nothing left to see behind you. Just keep going forward.

It must have snowed recently as the snow on the pavement is still fresh and so the descent of the hill not as treacherous as the ascent, when the hill was covered in black ice. I walk past an open window behind thick, black iron bars. I overhear the angry, raised voices met by one of protest which I had heard earlier down the corridor. I say a little prayer for the helpless man whose turn it's now to be, no doubt, subjected to a similar treatment that I had been, if not, quite possibly, worse.

I get to the bottom of the hill. There are no souls about, no cars either. But there, far away, at the horizon, to the left I can just about perceive a bustling street. That's where the city centre must be. That's where I'm headed! I carry on through the desolate landscape, only the silhouette of a church and a few buildings, a few houses, here and there. I catch sight of my reflection again in a window and I notice that my face is still dirty. I resolve to find somewhere to sit down for a moment and clean my face properly. Moments later I come across a rock and decide to take a bit of time, catch my breath and clean my face with some of the fresh snow, which is what I do. The snow feels bitter cold on my face but the sun is still shining a little which makes the experience bearable. I sit there for a while to regain some strength and try to figure out how to get home. Maybe an hour's walk or so, to where I could see the bustling street. And then, when I'll get there, I'll just ask someone which would be the right bus to get on, to get home. And that's how I'll get home.

The sun's gone in now and it's starting to get chilly. I look around me and realise that I am pretty much on the edge of a building site. But it's not just any building site. It's the building site of Ceausescu's monument of epic megalomania – the People's House. One of the main reasons for the never ending misery, poverty and lack endured by the people who had never asked, requested nor demanded its construction nor wished to carry the burden for it. Covering an enormous immensity of space with the final phase, by the looks of it, nowhere near, I feel small, insignificant, like an ant in comparison to its huge scale. But then again, I guess that was Ceausescu's intended motivation and purpose for it after all. "Oh look how small and meaninglessness you all are whilst here I am, stood at its balcony, God-like, looking down upon you!" Alas, he never lived to see its completion!

My moment of rest and contemplation is interrupted by the sound of an approaching engine. I jump up straight away as a quick thought is forming in my head. I run up towards the main road and reach it just as I see the car, a taxi, turning the corner coming towards me. I instinctively put my hand up and the taxi skids to a stop a few meters ahead. I quickly run up to it before he gets a chance to drive off, open the door and get in on the back seat. I figure that, if I'm already in, the taxi driver might think twice about getting rid of me. I give him the address, he looks at me in the rear view mirror but doesn't say anything. He nods and drives off. It's fairly warm inside and I relax a little.

"What day is it?" I ask him but almost regret it immediately because who wouldn't know what day it was? I don't want to raise his suspicions and for him to change his mind about taking me home.

He looks at me in the mirror, curiously, but answers nevertheless. "Monday."

I'm getting really warm inside the taxi now and decide to take my hat off. And as my hat comes off, I catch a glimpse of myself in the rear view mirror and wish I hadn't done so. The top of my head, where the forehead meets the hairline, is caked in blood. I quickly put my hat back on before drawing the taxi driver's attention to it. I don't want to have to answer any questions. I just want to get home. And since we are now well on our way, for the first time I allow myself to think of my little sister and the prospect of seeing her little face in a short while, and my mum, my grandmother and perhaps my great-grandma, too. I can't wait to see them all, to hug them tight and to tell them how grateful I am to have survived this ordeal, if only for this moment!

We are now in the thick of the city, a bustling place with what seems like thousands of people going about their daily business like they always do, like they've always done. Life like they've always known it. Only mine has been so drastically altered over the past few days, weeks, months... Still, I feel elated to be surrounded by the liveliness of the city, the excitement making me both high and exhausted in equal measure.

The taxi driver keeps on driving, looking from time to time in his rear view mirror. At first, I think he's staring at me but after a while I realise that in fact, he is looking at my coat. A thick, warm, navy, red and white jacket which, despite its current dirtiness and possibly smelliness, is nevertheless still stylish and attractive.

Outside, the sky has suddenly become dark with heavy clouds and I'm sure it can't be long until the snow will start falling. I can recognise that we are now driving along the main road, not far from my mum's house. The taxi then turns a corner into a side road, pulls to the kerb and here we are, at home!

"I have to run in and get some money for you from my mum," I tell the taxi driver, "but I'll leave you my coat so that you know that I'll be back shortly."

He doesn't say anything but nods and so seems to agree with the arrangement.

I get out of the taxi, take my coat off, throw it on the back seat and run into the house. It's so wonderful to finally be home. I'm hoping at least my mum or my grandma would be here though I wish everyone else was, too, as I just can't wait to see them all.

When I walk in, the house is so quiet though, I start to question if anyone at all is at home. I start shouting out their names, "Mum, Mutti! I'm home!"

All of a sudden, I hear some muffled commotion in the living room, where the door is shut. The door slowly opens and my grandma peeks her head round the door. She sees me but looks, for a moment, as if she's seen a ghost. She blinks a few times, then upon realising that it is actually me, she shrieks in delight and runs up to hug me. "Diana! My Diana!"

I'm so happy to feel my grandma's warm embrace and kisses, I start laughing and crying with joy at the same time. "She's here! Diana's home!" she shouts behind her and soon enough my little sister, whom I wasn't even sure would even be here, comes out of the living room. We run to each other and I scoop her up in a bear hug and cover her in kisses.

"You smell!" she laughs as she pretends to push me away. She is shortly followed by my great-grandmother who starts crying quietly as she hugs me.

"You're here as well?" I ask.

"Yes," my grandma answers. "We decided to regroup. Thought it best if we were all together in one place for a while."

"Where's Mum?" I ask Mutti.

"Ah! Your mum!" she says waving her hand as if annoyed. "I told her you're not dead! She wouldn't listen to me... The doctor had to come to see to her in the end.

Because, you know, Gina came to my place on Friday and she was crying and screaming hysterically. Saying 'They killed her! They killed my girl!' I didn't believe it! Not for one second! Still, I couldn't calm her down. In the end, I had to call her doctor friend. She came and gave her an injection to calm her down a little. Which she did, eventually. Then we all came back here, but she has locked herself in her room ever since then. She didn't think she would see you again, that you'd come back. She's refusing to come out of the bedroom…" It takes me a few seconds to register what my grandma had just said.

"She thought I was dead? They told her that they had killed me?" I ask Mutti, confused as to why that might be the case.

"Yes," Mutti continues. "After they brought her in to see you in that room, they told her to wait outside. Then after a few minutes, that Vasile monster went up to her and told her that he'd killed you and that Gina would have to go home and wait for your coffin…"

I try to take in what my grandma is telling me. It's hard for my heart not to break in a million pieces as I think of what torment my mum must have felt upon hearing those cruel words. Now I finally understand why mum had been nowhere to be seen when I was escorted out of the interrogation room by those two women, when I searched with my eyes the corridor for her. And also, why she hadn't come to see me when I was incarcerated, either. She must have been sent home by then, taken their word for granted – and why shouldn't she, given the experiences she and my grandma had had at their hands… But my thoughts are interrupted by the sound of a car horn.

"The taxi driver! Mutti, I need some money to pay him! He's still waiting outside!" my grandma then rushes towards the entrance hall, and grabs her handbag. She opens it and gets a few notes out of her purse.

"Oh, my goodness, you quickly go and pay him – I'm wearing slippers!" she says. I take the money from her hand and rush out of the door.

Outside, the driver is waiting with the engine running. He opens the car window, I give him the money, which he takes and pockets without even counting. He thanks me and says he's glad I got home safe.

I thank him, too, for having got me here safely. I tell him that I would like him to have my coat, but it no doubt needs a good clean to be at its best. He says a quiet "God bless" and waves goodbye. I stand on the pavement for a bit and watch as the car pulls off and disappears in the traffic.

Just as I'm about to turn around and head back indoors, the atmosphere becomes eerily quiet and then all of a sudden, snow starts to fall. Big, fat snowflakes covering my face, my jumper, my jeans. I close my eyes and stretch out my arms, breathing in the moment of magic I had promised myself to enjoy in that taxi all those days ago on my way to that forsaken place. I stay in this moment for a while. Just breathing. Just being. Being grateful. What for? For everything and for nothing in particular. Just feeling grateful.

Eventually, I open my eyes. The street lamps are now on and I watch mesmerised the snowflakes playing in the light. I look up above, give a wink and whisper a thank you for I take this to be not just my magic moment and a moment of gratitude but also my moment of blessing from above.

I run back inside where the smell of food in the house, delicious food, reminds me that I have not eaten properly in days. But firstly, I rush up the stairs to my mum's bedroom and push open the door. Curtains drawn, the room is in total darkness.

"Mum," I say softly. "I'm home."

I hear her stirring, fumbling a bit and then a bed side lamp flickers on. The light is faint and my mum squints to look at me, propping herself up on one elbow. Her hair is a mess, her eyes, with dark circles underneath, look bloodshot and she looks at me bewildered, full of confusion.

"Mum, it's me," I say again as I walk slowly towards her side of the bed. I sit down on the bed and touch her arm. "I'm home, Mum."

She looks at my hand which is resting on her arm and then at me again, incredulously, as she starts to say, "How can it be? They said you…"

"I know what they said. Mutti told me. But they lied. I'm home now."

She smiles faintly, nods her head and closes her eyes again, resting her head back down on the pillow. "Go and take a shower. You stink!" she says.

I smile to myself as I realise that she must be already getting back to her old self.

I leave her room and go to the bathroom. I switch the shower on – there is hot water! Another small miracle! I find a plastic bag in one of the cabinet drawers, open it and place it on the floor. I start taking my clothes off and stuffing them in the bag, one by one, as they come off. I look at my reflection in the mirror and I notice the cut at the top of the forehead, dry blood all around it and in my hair, too. The place where the barrel of the gun was against my head when I had pulled the trigger. I take my jumper and vest off and I catch sight of a huge bruise covering my entire left shoulder. I instinctively turn to take a look at my back, suspecting that it is also covered in an array of bruises, but stop myself before I can see any of the damage. I don't want to see it. I don't want to give these bruises any power. Or the people who had caused them. Or the ordeal I had been through. I refuse to do it. Only I have power over the significance of my life. I say it over and over again. Drowning all other thoughts that might be crossing my mind, trying to own my own power.

I get into the shower and stand under it, enjoying its warmth. Water. Sacred water. I see all the dirt mixed with blood being rushed down the drain as I wash myself and my hair, too. I feel cleansed. All the dirt gone, all the humiliation gone, all the degradation gone. *This is where it ends,* I think to myself. Down the drain. And this is where a new beginning starts. Like the tough strong woman, that my great-grandma told me once that I was, all those months ago. Facing with dignity and integrity whatever life would bring me. Because I can take it.

The shower starts getting cold, so I switch it off. I get out and put a towel around me. I'm now famished so I'm already thinking about eating some of the delicious food my grandma is cooking for me, then playing with my sister, meeting up with friends and messing around, having fun with them, going back to school, getting back to living my life.

And so, the following day, back to my grandma's home and to the daily routine again, time passes quickly. Days, then weeks and then months. After my interrogation, arrest and release, my mother gets summoned to be interrogated less and less frequently. The surveillance is still in place, though. A different kind of more subtle abuse is taking place with her receiving unjustified yet frequent admonishment at work, a thinly veiled attempt of being bullied out of her place of work which she refuses to give in to. Moreover, her boss, the one administering the admonishments walks her to the bus stop one day and explains himself for treating her in this manner, "What can I do? My hands are tied. If I don't do as I'm asked they'll see me out of the job..." he tells her by way of an apology.

"Of course. I know and I've known from the first time you started being critical of my work. No hard feelings," my mum would reassure him.

Similar situations would occur to me at school, too. On more than one occasion I would give answers to questions my maths teacher would ask, to be told that my answers were wrong only for another student to give the exact same answer and be rewarded for it. I mean, maths! You either get it right or wrong, little room for ambiguity.

The situation became so obvious that following one too many such incidences, the whole class even realised that I was being unfairly treated. As a result, the students started to take to either bursting into laughter or just clapping whilst shouting, "Well done, such as such, for giving exactly the same answer as Diana has just done a second ago!" the teacher would shout back at the students to quiet down or face detention.

On another occasion, whilst we were having a double literature lesson, a similar thing had happened with the teacher praising another pupil for having given the same answer as I had done myself a few seconds previously. As a result, the whole class got up and walked out, including the student who had given the answer. I remained sat behind, watching them bemused as they all filed out one by one, in protest, looking at the teacher in disgust as they walked past her. The teacher was raving and threatening them all, which obviously fell on deaf ears.

Eventually, she sat down behind her desk, head in her hands, looking dejected and desolate. It was just myself and her left in the classroom, and for a second I even felt sorry for her. But then, I took into account that not all the teachers were treating me as such, remembering my French teacher and my art teacher who were always fair to me. Which made me conclude that the ones who weren't had probably opted to do so, all too eager to endear themselves to the security services and their requests.

In the end, when her head came up and she looked at me, I simply said to her with a twinkle in my eye, "I guess this game is over. And it looks like I won. Without even intending to." She looked absolutely furious because she knew she could no longer carry on the charade.

But all she managed to say to me was, "Get out of my classroom, you little bitch!"

I wasn't going to turn down the opportunity of getting out of school a bit earlier, though before leaving her classroom I couldn't resist telling her that, "I think you might have just determined me to become a teacher. So I can end up being everything that you are not." Needless to say that I didn't hang around for a reaction!

Another thing that happened after my arrest and release is that one of the girls, Dani, who had become an almost inseparable best friend, started turning up, whenever we would get together, with this guy on tow. She introduced him as a university colleague, though he looked much older than her, and when I asked them if they were an item she laughed so hard I dismissed the idea straight away. So why was he always hanging around us? Well, the answer came one early morning when I saw my friend out of the window, leaving for university. I can't remember why, but I was starting school later that particular day and upon seeing her by herself for once, I thought I was going to confront her about him. I quickly ran out of the flat, out of the building and called her name before she would disappear. Upon hearing me, she stopped, furtively glanced up and down the street, and quickly grabbed me by the arm. Then, she walked me back into the building where she called the lift, and still without saying one word, bundled me in and pressed the top floor button. In the lift she simply said, "We'll talk in a minute," and so when the lift stopped, I followed her out. And then I fell behind her steps again as she tiptoed up some stairs to a floor I didn't even know existed. There, at the far end of the corridor was a door with a latch on it. She unhooked the latch and opened the door which, as it happened, led onto the rooftop of the building. We step outside, a flat rooftop with an amazing bird's-eye view of Bucharest. It was a clear day and you could easily see from the TV tower to the dome cupola of the National Library and the National University. How did I not know that this place existed and how did she even know of it?

"It used to be my secret hidey place when I was a teenager and needed a place to get away from everyone. And have a sneaky cigarette without anyone knowing..." she says sheepishly as she lights up one.

"Nobody will find us up here and I doubt it very much if anyone would be able to overhear our conversation up here. So here goes it: that freak, who's been hanging around and calls himself my friend, is a *Securitate* agent. Together with another guy, someone older, they came and paid me and my mum a visit a couple of weeks ago. Told mum that if I don't do as I'm told they'd have me thrown out of university. When I told them that they wouldn't have a reason to kick me out, given how I'm a straight 'A' student, they said that they'd find a reason, and if they couldn't, they'd make one up. They also threatened that they wouldn't allow for my brother's passport to be issued and that way he wouldn't be able to join his new wife in France."

My friend's brother, had recently got married to a French lady, whom he had met whilst she was holidaying on the Black Sea a few years beforehand. Following the marriage, he had recently put forward an application for a passport and a request to be allowed to move to France with her, where they wanted to start their married life together. And now, this was being used as leverage so that a *Securitate* agent could obviously keep taps on me…

"We'll have to play along. Meet up openly once a week, talk bullshit in front of this guy but whenever we want to talk for real we'll do it up here from now on! We'll meet here every Friday evening at 7 pm, come what may, and we decide when we meet next during the week. Deal?"

"Deal!" I say. And from that day on, we do exactly just that!

A few more months pass and my mother receives an official letter informing her of a date and time for when my father's trial is to take place, in a military tribunal. The charges against him are high treason for trying to overthrow the communist government of Romania, desertion by defecting to a foreign, enemy nation, and undermining the economy of Romania in the international arena.

A few days thereafter, my mother receives another letter with a date and time for her own trial at the same military tribunal. She is being charged with conspiracy to my father's treason. My mother is outraged by the charge and starts to frantically search for a solicitor who would be willing to take on her case. Which, of course, is almost impossible to find, as at the mere mention of treason of the communist government she gets shunned straight away. Almost impossible. For eventually, she does find someone. Someone who is more than willing to take on her case and fight on her behalf. A retired solicitor and a close friend of my late grandfather's, my mother's father, who at 79 years of age is as lucid and fired up about the case as it can get. He gets down to business the moment he commits himself to the job, religiously taking three buses every single day to make the trip to and from his house to my mum's, in order to discuss every evening the details of the charges, the evidence and the defence strategy.

"Aren't you afraid?" I overhear my mum asking him one weekend. "That they'll try to harm you, to come after you, for defending traitors?" He takes his glasses off, raises an eyebrow, looks at her bemused, and takes her hand in his.

"Your father was a loyal, dear friend. We had a friendship which lasted a lifetime. And him, just like me, lived life honourably, with integrity, above all else. So if they'll come after me, it would an honour to go down defending 'traitors'."

Summer of 1989 finally arrives. After the long, heavy, freezing winter, it's a welcome feeling to enjoy the warm sunshine every day. But of course, the arrival of the summer months also heralds the approach of my parents' trials.

My father's first, which is to take place behind the closed doors of the Military Tribunal, for which besides my mother's solicitor, the only people allowed to attend are the tribunal president, the judge and the state assessors, aka, those charged with investigating the case of my father's defection, among them some of the people who had interrogated my mother and myself, too. Because it's a closed tribunal, my mother is not allowed to attend the trial but she has permission to be present when the sentencing is read.

She knows from lengthy conversations with her solicitor that there will be one likely outcome only. Indeed, this proves to be the case, on the 11th July, when the presiding officer of the tribunal, Gica Popa – do make a mental note as the name will yet again rear its ugly head in a few months' time – states: "It has been unanimously voted for Virgil Baleanu to be sentenced to death by firing squad and have the totality of his personal assets confiscated for the treason of sharing state secrets with enemy powers."

As expected as the sentencing turns out to be, my mum comes home devastated by its blow. She refuses to eat, refuses to talk to anyone and shuts herself in her bedroom. There are only a matter of days before her own trial is to take place and there is nothing that can persuade her to leave her bedroom.

She has even given up on going to work. On one occasion she asks me to get my little sister for her. I go to get her from wherever she is happily playing and take her to my mum's bedroom, to her side of the bed. My mum starts hugging her tight and would not let go of her. My sister gets restless and tries to wriggle out of my mum's arms but my mum would still not let go. My little sister then gets upset by it all and in the end I have to step in and grab her out of mum's tight embrace. "Mum stop it! You're scaring her," I snap at her but she just turns over in bed and faces the other way.

Soon after, my sister and I return to Mutti's flat because despite the summer holidays having just started, I find the atmosphere at my mum's house too depressing and distressing.

The day of my mum's trial and sentencing arrives and yet again is to take place behind closed doors. My grandma, my sister and I accompany my mum to the Tribunal but once she goes inside the court room with her solicitor, the door gets shut in our faces.

We wait and wait inside. It's the middle of the summer and the court house is oppressively and stiflingly hot. In the end, the three of us resolve to go outside, to wait on the steps outside the Tribunal for news of the unfolding events. The steps outside are under shade which is slightly more bearable than being indoors. Moreover, the stairs themselves feel quite cool so we all sit down, waiting. Just waiting. My sister gets restless so we start playing a game of hide and seek around the staircase. Meanwhile, a black car pulls up outside the building, just in front of the staircase, but no one gets out. The driver is keeping the engine running and I find the smell of petrol fumes unbearable.

We get up and decide to go back indoors when we hear commotion coming from inside the Tribunal. Then suddenly, the doors burst open and I see my mum dishevelled, trying to fight off the two men who, with a tight grip on both of her arms, are marching her down the stairs.

"My girls! My girls!" my mum cries at seeing us halfway up the stairs. "Please! Let me say goodbye to my girls! Please, just one second, that's all I ask for!"

Her plea falls on deaf ears as the two men on either side of her completely ignore her request and continue to march her on. My sister, upon seeing mum, runs up to her and grabs at her legs, her skirt but she is pushed off by one of the men. She falls to the floor and starts crying so I quickly scoop her up in my arms. My grandma is now following my mum and the two men down the stairs.

"Gina, what's going on? What's happening?" my grandma is shouting over my mum's cries, trying to get some information from her. Before we know what's happening, my mum is bundled into the back of the black waiting car, the two men get in on either side of her and the car speeds off. We are all stood frozen to the spot, right there on the courthouse steps, silent but for the soft cries coming from my little sister. Eventually, my mum's solicitor walks out of the courthouse door.

"What happened?" both myself and Mutti ask him at the same time.

"Conspiracy to treason. She was sentenced to seven years of hard labour. Starting immediately."

My grandma gives a shriek and slides down, collapsing on the stairs.

"What does that mean?" I ask the solicitor.

"Well, it means that your mum will be taken to a labour camp, far away from here. We have not been told where, yet," he says and hesitates about carrying on.

I had heard of such labour camps, the communist gulags of Romania but active in many other countries of the communist bloc, too, with the one in Siberia, Russia, being the most feared and notorious of them all. Places where political dissidents and hardened criminals were sent to spend their sentences, never to actually see them through given how the conditions were so harsh, that most people sent there would not come back alive.

I am too numb to react. To cry. To feel anything. Still holding my little sister in my arms, I lend my grandma a hand to help get her up.

"Let's go home, Mutti. There's nothing left for us here."

We take the bus back to my mum's house as it's agreed that it's cooler there than the greenhouse which has become my grandma's flat, given the soaring temperatures.

As soon as we get there, we all retreat to different parts of the house, trying to piece together the events of the past few hours, the past few weeks and months and trying to make sense of the months to come.

The window in my bedroom is open and a light breeze drifts in. I am laying on my bed, staring at this one spot on the wall. Outside, I hear children playing, cars driving, birds chirping. "How can they?" I ask myself. "How can life just carry on as if no seismic change had occurred?" But of course, the change is only felt by us – me, my sister, Mutti and my mum, wherever she might be by now...

Hours pass and I'm still staring at the wall in my bedroom. The sun has now gone down, outside there are less and less cars to be heard. Less children playing, too. I hear my grandma pottering around in the kitchen, moving pots and pans. She comes into my bedroom and asks gently, "Would you two girls like to come and have some dinner?"

I look over to where my sister is deep asleep next to me. I don't even have the energy to shake my head. So I just carry on staring at this one spot on the wall. I'm afraid that if I stop, if I take my focus away for one tiny micro second, my world might fall irretrievably apart.

My grandma looks at me, then at my sister, but doesn't say anything else, anymore; just quietly shuts the door behind her. I wonder if my body will ever be able to function again, if it will know how to. I think of my little sister, right here in front of me. She will grow up without mum, she will never get to know her, will probably even forget her in time...

Night time falls. The house is deadly quiet, outside all of the voices of children long since gone. Occasionally, I hear a TV being switched on somewhere in the vicinity, in someone's house, a random bus or a random car engine drifting past. I think about sleeping, but I can't. I can't close my eyes. I can't stop staring at this one spot on the wall...

I hear some more noise coming from the front of the house. My grandmother pottering around again. *She must have popped out earlier and was now getting back,* I absently think to myself.

"Ma," I hear a voice calling somewhere and for a second I think it is my mum's. *Who am I kidding?* I sigh without moving. *Probably someone next door calling their mum. Or perhaps, I'm just hearing things – it must happen when you wish so hard for someone to be there.*

"Ma!" I hear it again, clearer and nearer, and this time I shoot straight up in bed. *What the...?* I rub my eyes, jump out of the bed and go to investigate.

The whole house is in darkness. I start walking down the corridor towards the front of the house and then the dining room lights switch on.

"Mum?" I say, not quite believing my eyes. *Have I fallen asleep? Am I dreaming? Hallucinating? I must be.* But, sure as anything, my mum is right here, walking towards me, tired smile on her face. I stand fixed to the spot, still unsure as to what is happening. My mum comes up, squeezes my arm with a weak smile as she walks past on her way to the bathroom.

"It's really you?" I ask after her, beyond bewildered.

"Yes, I'm back," she says from beyond the bathroom door.

I am still stunned but I realise that my grandma obviously doesn't know that mum is back, so I start going round the house looking for her. She's not in the living room, not in her bedroom. The kitchen lights are off. Where is she?

"Mutti!" I call her as I put some water on boil for some tea, in the kitchen. Still no sign of her. I get some cups out and tea leaves, too, and start making the tea. Eventually Mutti walks in.

"Where have you been?" I ask her possibly a bit too harshly as she is taken aback by my tone.

"Oh, I didn't think you'd be up again, I thought you were out for the night. I went to the back of the house to have a cigarette…" she says sheepishly.

"Mum is back," I blurt out.

"What? Gina's back?" she asks but before I have a chance to reconfirm it, my mother walks in.

"Yes, I'm back. Thank God! Thank God! Thank God!"

Mum opens the fridge door, gets some food out, Mutti gets her a plate and then we all sit down round the kitchen table.

"What happened?" I ask. My mum takes a few bites of a sandwich, a sip of her tea and puts the cup down.

"After you saw what happened at the tribunal, they threw me in the back of that car and drove me to the train station. The car stopped just outside of the train station, they put handcuffs on my wrists. I told them it wasn't necessary that I wasn't going to run off anywhere. They wouldn't listen. Not that they were putting the cuffs on so that I wouldn't run. It was just done to degrade me. We got out of the car, they grabbed my arms again and they frogmarched me to a train. Everyone we walked past at the train station stopped and stared. The cuffs were on full view, they pretty much paraded me around the station. They already had the tickets in their pockets, so they pushed me on the train, and then they got on themselves, right behind me. They sat me down, they went out for a cigarette and then returned and took their seats next to mine.

"The train started the pull off. They didn't talk to me and I didn't say a word to them, either. What could I have said? The hand was dealt, the cards had fallen… I kept looking out of the window thinking that maybe I could see any of you… But, of course, you weren't to know where they had taken me… Half an hour must have passed since the train had left the station at Bucharest, when one of them started talking, saying, 'You'll die serving your sentence there, you know. No woman survives seven years of hard labour.' I carried on looking out of the window, trying to ignore him, trying to shut him out…"

She stops and takes another bite of her sandwich, another sip of her tea.

"'You'll never see your children again,' he carried on. Still trying to ignore him. I didn't want to give the bastards the satisfaction of seeing my tears. They didn't deserve it. 'Your children will grow up without a mother. And your own mother will probably be dead by the time your seven years will be up, even if you will survive the hard labour. Then, your children will be taken into an orphanage. Probably different ones too, given their age gap...' I turned and spat him right in the face. Couldn't help myself.

"A few good minutes passed before the other one started talking, '...it doesn't have to be this way, you know. There is another way, of course.' *Another way?* I thought to myself. *What other way could there be? I have been tried and sentenced?* I looked at him curiously. He continued talking, taking out an envelope from his breast pocket. 'We could take your cuffs off and you could sign this. In return, we suspend your sentence.' What on earth could they want me to sign now? I tried to figure out. Virgil is sentenced to death, all his assets taken... His fate has been sealed as has my own... 'What do you want me to sign?' I asked him. Anyhow, he opened the envelope, took out a piece of paper out of it, unfolded it and placed it in front of me. 'Divorce papers,' he answered. 'You divorce Virgil and then, sign a testimony saying that you never wish to be associated with him again in any capacity. And to show leniency, we suspend your sentence, you go back home to your children and you get to keep your job. You will have sole custody of the children. You carry on with your life. All ends well.' He concluded.

"So, their offer needed no consideration. I brought my arms up on the table, allowed them to take the cuffs off, took the pen and signed the damn documents. What else could I have done?" she finishes, shrugging her shoulders.

"But, this means..." my grandma starts saying before being interrupted by my mum.

"Yes, I know, there is no more hope of ever seeing him again now. For me or the girls. It was either that or the children ending up without ever seeing either of their parents again. At least, this way, I get to see them grow up. And then who knows what the future might hold for them..." my mum answers somewhat defensively.

So, this is it, then... I try to take in the latest twist in the developments. How we will probably never hear nor see my father again. And then, I think how only a few minutes ago I was hoping for a miracle to happen so that my mum could be safe, so that she would return, so I could see her again, and now here she was. And for that, regardless of the circumstances, I was grateful. It was, without any doubt, the only thing that truly mattered.

"Mum, don't worry, you did the right thing, the only thing you could have done," I say as a way to reassure her.

She looks at me, though it seems that she's looking more through me than at me. I can tell that she's disappointed, disillusioned, distressed at the way things have turned out. But. But! Can we finally trust that the living nightmare which has been our lives for too long now, can finally be put behind us? For, with a death sentence given to my father, the government has ensured that he would never return to the country and then by divorcing my parents and giving my mother full custody of us, her children, the government also ensured that my father can never see any of us again. The vendetta done, the ultimate revenge accomplished. Nothing else left to be done.

And so, had it all been in vain? I can't help but ask myself. No change brought about for the people, who continue to endure living in appalling conditions, no change to the status quo of the country leadership, to the life of anyone other than the pain, the suffering, the abuse and now the definitive family separation endured by us, as a family. Was any of it worth anything at all? Will the wounds ever heal? Will time tell? My pensiveness is shortly interrupted by my little sister walking in, rubbing her eyes sleepily. She walks up to mum and settles on her lap, in her arms, quickly falling asleep again, oblivious to the fact that mum was only a few hours ago about to go out of our lives possibly forever...

November 1989

1989. An exceptional year which unexpectedly changed the shape of history and reshaped the geo-political map of Europe. 1989. The year of the collapse of the Eastern Communist Bloc. The year which saw the opposition party in Poland victorious at elections, Hungary adopting political pluralism, Erich Honecker ousted from the leadership of the Democratic Republic of Germany and on the 9th November, the Berlin Wall, that ultimate symbol of European division between western democracy and eastern socialist totalitarianism, being taken down brick by brick by Berliners. The movement continued to sweep across Eastern Europe into December, too, with a non-Communist government coming into power in Czechoslovakia and even in our neighbouring Bulgaria, Mladenov, a liberal, replacing the communist Jivkov.

At home, none of us dare to listen to any of the pro-democracy radio stations and by the beginning of December, no mention of the events above are made on national TV or radio. But, news always has a way of traveling. People talk. And, boy are they talking in Bucharest! Heck, they are talking of nothing else! In the queue at the bakery, in the market, in the street, at the bus stop, even at my school, the kids are now starting the day's conversation with, "Have you heard...?" News is traveling fast all around us and it's impossible to be stopped.

Personally, I feel more and more quietly angered by every report and mention of yet another communist government being toppled. It seems like each and every communist government around Romania is crashing down, all but Romania's.

I still meet with my best friend, Dani, on top of my grandma's building on a regular basis. Her brother has left Romania and is now well and truly settled in Nice, in the South of France. My friend, she is now engaged herself to an Italian friend of her brother's and is hoping to be married next summer.

One day, when we meet up, I share my indignation at the lack of any hint of political change in Romania, despite the wave of change all around the Eastern bloc.

"All these countries have found the courage to take a stand and see change through. Why isn't Romania standing up to its tyrants?"

"Bah!" she'd answer. "Nobody to organise anything over here. The Romanians have never been great at taking charge. That's why we ended up with a foreign king leading us, not so long ago."

"Or is it that the Romanians are too fond of Ceausescu and quite content with the way things are?" I'd answer back.

"Oh, c'mon, you've been hearing the same noise as everyone else, the constant, daily mumblings at every street corner, for years now. You know that's not the case."

"I know, I know. Still, that's just words. Nobody's doing anything…" I'd say. And so we'd go on and on, backward and forwards for hours, both of us, venting, during those long, dark evenings of the beginning of December 1989.

And then, one morning, the mood of the city changes. It's as if I can sense the change even before hearing any of the day's news. There seems to be a new complicity in the eyes of every passer-by, a different energy in their step and their demeanour.

"What's the latest?" I ask my friend as I bump into her at the bus stop, on our way to our respective schools. She smiles and winks at me and nods in the direction of some guy, a few steps away, who's holding court at the bus stop, regaling those waiting for the bus with the latest news.

"…It's started. That's it. The beginning of the end, mark my words. In Timisoara, yesterday, my sister who lives over there, phoned me and told me, that there were thousands of people out in the street. Shouting their support for Laszlo Tokes, you know, the pastor who's been criticising Ceausescu. Give it a few days and I'm sure of it, it will kick off even here, in Bucharest, as well!"

We're all looking at him, enrapt, mouths literally open, as if he's telling a fantastic fable story. His story is only punctuated by some in the crowd saying, "Wow!", "You hear that?", "That's amazing."

Though one or two people do say, "Hush down, you might never know which ones among us might be Securitate Officers, then you'll end up in prison…" But, the man is not to be deterred.

"Oh, we've been quiet for long enough. It's time to make some noise, time to finally make ourselves heard."

That said, the bus arrives and the crowd scatters. It's one of the last days of school and so my friend and I make plans to meet up on the first day of the holidays to have lunch out with some of her friends.

On my way back from school I pick up my sister from her school. Back at the flat, both my great-grandmother and Mutti are there. Mutti now spends more of her time with us at her flat than with mum, at mum's place, since now, following the trial and its outcome, my mum is no longer randomly arrested and since her divorce from my dad has been granted, she no longer fears for her life. Evening falls, the TV is on in the background and Mutti has just asked me to set up the dinner table. I'm pottering around the dining table when the phone rings. I go to pick it up.

"Hello?" I say.

"Hello, sweetheart," I hear a voice at the other end of the line and my heart skips a beat. It can't be! But it must be. Clear as daylight. Crisp voice. Perfect connection. I sit myself down, unsure as to what to say next. What do you say, to someone you haven't heard from in two years? Two years, which seem to have lasted for two lifetimes.

"Hi, Dad. How are you doing?" I answer back, despite the hundreds of other things I want to say, the hundreds of questions I have for him…

"Yes, I'm good. But, how are you? And Anna?"

Mmm. How am I? Just like that, as if he'd just left for work this morning and he is just calling to check in. How am I? How do you sum up two years of separation, of anguish, of uncertainty, of pain in a phone call?

"Yes, fine, we're both fine. Just fine. How did you know we were here?" I ask, for something to say.

"I called home earlier. Mum said you were here."

I reply with a short, "Oh," and an awkward silence follows.

Then I hear him talking again at the other end of the line, "You'll have to start packing soon, the time is almost there for us to be together again."

I don't quite know how to respond nor what would make him say this. So, in the end we say our goodbyes but not before he promises to call again soon. I hang up and as I do my attention is caught by something on the TV screen.

Ceausescu is on the telly with the words breaking news or special communique or something as such, flashing from time to time at the bottom of the screen. I go to turn up the volume and sink in a chair in front of the TV captivated by what I hear. Ceausescu is giving a speech condemning the 'hooligans' who had recently been out on the streets of Timisoara and who acted in a 'terrorist' manner. I had heard earlier in the day, on my way back from school, snippets of information about how the military had opened fire on the thousands of people peacefully protesting in Timisoara and now, listening to Ceausescu's speech I naively believe for a second that he is condemning the actions of the military. But then, he carries on demonising those who had 'lined the streets of Timisoara, having been organised by foreign security and spying services in order to sell their country' and how the army had had to step in 'to fulfil its duty' and then I quickly realise the implication.

However, I also realise that by addressing the issue on national TV he is turning something which up to now had been nothing but a rumour into an actual fact and thus is giving the uprising in Timisoara legitimacy. So now the whole country knows that all the street corner whisperings are true! Is he even aware that he's doing so? And with him doing so, will it cower the rest of the country into submission or will now the floodgates of dissent and protest burst open never to be closed again?

Mutti walks into the dining room and starts telling me off for having done nothing towards setting up the dinner table but wasting time instead. I point to the telly and she sits herself down for a second to watch it, but the speech is now at the end so I have to fill in the details for her. And about Dad's phone call, too. We sit there together like that for a few moments unsure as to what all of this might mean for us, for the family. And then we look at each other and smile in complicity as we both think the same thing and say at the same time, "Not long now!"

If over the past few weeks, people had been talking about the events sweeping Eastern Europe mainly in hushed voices, the following day, everybody is talking loudly and openly about the events of the past couple of days in Romania. Everywhere I'd go, everyone I'd walk past, would be unrestrainedly talking about Timisoara and democracy and bringing down the tyranny of the country. I mean, if Ceausescu had been talking about it on national TV why wouldn't the rest of the country? Albeit, with a different tone and meaning…

It's now the first day of the school holidays, and my friend, Dani and I had made plans to go out for lunch and celebrate being free from school for a few weeks. We meet up in front of my grandma's building and we make our way to the bus stop. Luckily, the weird guy who'd normally accompany her for our outings is nowhere to be seen. Sweet! We jump on the bus, there are only a few stops up the road to the cafe.

We chat away, happy to be in each other's company, but, just one bus stop short of our destination, the bus loops round a roundabout, narrowly avoiding a deviation road sign. *What the…? What's going on?* Everyone on the bus is mumbling in annoyance but the driver simply says, "I'm only following the rules, I don't get to make them…" The bus comes to a halt and we are all asked to get off, which we do.

There is only a short walk to where the café is, where we are supposed to meet my friend's colleagues. Since all the traffic is deviated, we decide to take a walk to it. We hear some people mentioning something about 'Ceausescu's meeting' and I recall my mother having said the previous evening, on the phone, that she and everyone else at her place of work – alongside everyone else with a place of work anywhere in Bucharest – had been summoned to attend a meeting at which Ceausescu was to give a speech. Since the meeting place was not far from Mutti's place, she said that she would try to pop in afterwards, before all of us would be going back to her house in time for the Christmas celebrations. But when mum had said meeting, for some reason, I had envisaged an indoors meeting, but now it occurs to me that Ceausescu was probably holding one of his frequent, large scale, public meetings, in an open space, outside some government building from which he would address the crowds as he would from time to time, in order to remind his people how fortunate they were to have him as a leader. Or some other such rhetoric.

It's a beautiful, sunny, crisp winter's day and quite unusually for this time of year, it hasn't snowed yet. We are walking towards the café, and I'm talking and talking, going on how Timisoara must be suffering and bleeding, and how despite it all, so disappointingly and heartbreakingly, nothing is happening in Bucharest. No support for Timisoara. No sign of change. Just people talking. Like they always do, like they've always done. All words, no action!

We are still walking, getting closer and closer to the main road, Magheru, and my friend is timidly asking me to stop talking. "Hush for a moment, will you?"

Thinking that she's doing so only because she doesn't want anyone to overhear us being critical of the government, I keep on talking. Infuriated. On and on I go. Everybody else is talking, why shouldn't I? Isn't it time we make ourselves heard, loud and clear? Until, my friend who has obviously had enough, turns around and snaps at me, "If you could just shut up for one second, then you might just be able to hear what I suspect to be the very voices of protest you are so desperately hoping to hear!"

Finally and startled by her outburst, I am shocked into silence. We both slow right down and listen.

And there it is! Faint, at first, almost like the sound of the wind. But then it gets louder and louder. Angrier and angrier. Clearer and clearer. Ceausescu's meeting, only a few steps away from where we are. The chanting, which should have been in support of him and his government and his leadership, has now turned against him, has turned into one of angry protest.

Bucharest has at long last heard the rest of Eastern Europe, has finally heard Timisoara, has once and for all had enough of Ceausescu and his speeches and everything he stood for and was now saying so loud and clear. The floodgates have opened!

We turn the corner from George Enescu into the Magheru Boulevard, not quite knowing what to expect. Nevertheless, nothing could have prepared us for the scene taking place before our eyes. A mass of people, walking down the middle of the avenue, away from the meeting, breaking up placards, throwing flags to the side of the road, to a deafening chant of, "Down with Ceausescu! Death to the criminal!"

My friend and I stop and stare. Incredulous and open mouthed at first but then we turn to face each other, jump and down, hugging each other, wiping tears of joy and relief but mostly of hope. "Our Christmas present has come early!"

And then, without hesitating for a second, we join the crowds, walking alongside them. My friend spots some friends from university who quickly bring us among their ranks, right in the heart of this mass of people. We keep on walking towards Piata Romana, round the roundabout and we loop back again. But as we do so, we notice that army groups with tanks and army vehicles are closing in, some from side roads off the Magheru Boulevard, and then a larger group of army soldiers and tanks coming from our opposite direction.

It looks like we are trapped from all corners and all directions. Many of the shops lock their doors, bring down their shutters. Some others, send their assistants out with water and food for the crowds, I guess in solidarity.

We had come to a standstill almost next to Tache Ionescu, a lateral, side road where a tank with about four soldiers and an officer have parked up and are now sat atop the tank, smoking, watching the crowds. The soldiers are not much older than myself, maybe one or two years older. They look visibly shook up at finding themselves in the situation in which they now are. Some of the people in the crowds try to engage them. "What are you boys going to do? Shoot us? The army's duty is to protect its people, not the politicians."

The soldiers together with the officer look uncomfortable and fidget around, not making eye contact with anyone in the crowd. None of them engage with the public. I wonder how many of their parents, brothers and sisters, their own family, might be among the crowds. Maybe not this particular crowd but one of the many other ones which we hear that have formed once Ceausescu's meeting's crowd split up, going in different directions of the Magheru Boulevard. And I also wonder if, when it came to it, the soldiers who were expected to shoot at the people would fail to do so, if they themselves would not be shot for refusing to follow orders?

We keep chatting and, from time to time, chanting. A while later, something like a light flickers in a shop window and catches my eye. I look up trying to figure out where the light is coming from. I see movement on the rooftop of the buildings opposite us. I keep watching, looking up and a few other people see me doing so and start looking up themselves. Yes, sure enough, snipers are now taking their positions on rooftops. A few people in the crowd panic, give out a loud gasp and some even try to dive for cover at the realisation, perhaps thinking that the snipers are just about to shoot at us. However, as soon as it becomes obvious that they are just taking their positions and they are not imminently going to shoot, people start to once again resume their chit chat, their chanting, making plans for the next steps of the protest.

It's getting late in the day, the sun is starting to come down and as there are no other developments taking place at the very moment, my friend and I decide to go back home, have some food, wrap up warmer and come back out later on with renewed energy. We're not sure how we will make our way home since all exists and roads are blocked by the military. We inch closer to Piata Romana, walk around the roundabout until we notice a gap between a tank and the pavement, right past the ASE building, where other people keep coming and going unobstructed, too.

"Let's walk past the tank, quickly. No eye contact with anyone," I say.

My friend agrees and says, "If anything, the army probably wants people to leave this place and never come back. Hopefully we should be OK."

We do as said, but just as we walk past the tank and its soldiers, one of them starts calling after us. "Miss, excuse me!"

Both my friend and I look at each other panicked and quickly grasp hands tight. We turn around at the same time and face the one who had been calling after us.

"Miss, excuse me. I don't suppose you might have a spare cigarette?" he asks.

Sighing a sigh of relief, my friend, hand shaking, gets out her pack of cigarettes and hands it to him.

"All yours! Take them!" she says. He tips his hat and then we turn around to briskly continue our walk home.

"Oh, that was scary!" we say to each other, giggling nervously and shaking with fear at the same time, once we are out of earshot. As we walk towards home, we come across other groups of people, chanting and walking in the direction from which we were coming.

At home, the second I walk through the front door, both Mutti and my great-grandmother start on me, "Where have you been? We've been so worried. Do you have any idea what's happening out there?" I try not to smile or to let on that I had actually been part of what is happening out there for most of the day as I'm afraid that I might not be allowed out again, later on. So I just tell them that I'd been out for a pizza just round the corner with friends, like I was supposed to.

In the living room, the telly is on and it's broadcasting parts of Ceausescu's meeting and speech, no mention of the protests that resulted at the end of it. I have something to eat, a hot chocolate, I warm up a bit and then it's time I go back out again. I tell Mutti and Mammy a little white lie, for I know that otherwise there's no chance I'd be allowed to leave the house. So I tell them that I'm going to spend the evening at my friend's place.

"Whatever you do, just don't go out there. Not this evening. It's too dangerous," they both warn me and I nod like a good girl, knowing full well that I have no intention of following their advice. I wrap up warm and quickly run out of the door, before Mutti gets a chance to change her mind about letting me out of the house at all.

When I get downstairs, my friend is already waiting outside of the building. We decide to walk towards University Square, by the National Theatre where she heard from some friends that it's going to be the place where most people are to congregate this evening. It's quite a long walk from Calea Dorobantilor and on our way, we overhear a lot of other groups of people, young and old, some with young families, even with small children on tow. They are all talking about going in the same direction. I remember the tanks and military vehicles we saw earlier and can't help asking myself how sensible is for children to be brought into all of this. But then again, I ask myself how sensible is it for me to be out here, too, and so, who am I to judge?

We get closer and closer to the square and in doing so we start to hear the chanting. Booming, loud chanting. Which makes us expect to see a huge crowd when we get there. We are certainly not disappointed when the sea of people is finally within view as we reach the small hilltop in front of the National Theatre. Both my friend and I can't help but stop and look around us in absolute overawe and overwhelm. A sea of people, stretching as far as the eye can see, some holding candles, some holding homemade placards, some waving flags with the communist symbol cut out, some chanting, some openly wishing others a Merry Christmas, some chatting quietly, smoking, chanting again. We walk around, sometimes joining in the chanting, sometimes just taking in the atmosphere. But mostly feeling so humbled and privileged to be able to be part of this moment. If we weren't sure earlier in the day, we know now for certain. There is no going back. The change talked about by my parents for so many years, is finally taking place right here, before our eyes. And this change is happening because the people are speaking out, they can no longer hold it in. This hardened, beaten down, long suffering people who can endure no more. The wish, the desire, the desperate need for change is resolute and so is this crowd's determination to see it happen no matter the cost. There is no going back now.

But, despite the amicable atmosphere of the crowd, there is also the underlying current of what might imminently happen. There is a large military presence with their tanks, further down from where we are, just to the side of the university building. And other large groups of army soldiers or possibly police officers wearing shields and most notably guns, are starting to close in from the different side roads of the square. People are starting to debate if the military would eventually open fire. Some are confidently stating that they certainly would, like they had done in Timisoara only a few nights ago. While others are arguing that given how the entire proceedings are being filmed by both the BBC and CNN from the windows of the Intercontinental hotel across the road, the army wouldn't dare do so, wouldn't dare to compromise the country's leadership on the international arena.

I notice that there are also a couple of ambulances parked not far from where the army and their tanks are stationed by the university building and remember Ceausescu's televised speech the previous day where he talked about the army 'having done their duty' in Timisoara. Will they also do their duty equally brutally here as well, I wonder. Will blood be shed? And for how long will the spilled blood manage to silence all the anger, the pain, the suffering endured for decades but which now can no more be contained?

My friend and I must have been here for a few hours already, now. The chanting is becoming more intense, louder, while the ever expanding crowd is becoming angrier. I'm just about to say something to my friend but my sentence gets drowned by what sounds like gunshots. People screaming. Panic. People running for cover. Where is the gunshot sound coming from? Are they real gunshots or just blanks meant to discourage people from being here? My friend and I reach out to each other, grasp hands and look at each other silently, eyes wide with dismay though frozen to the spot. We see a commotion by the side of the university building, more gunshots, more screaming and yet more commotion. It's not long before one of the ambulances turns on its siren and weaves its way through the crowds. It's obvious now that people have been wounded.

Yet, the crowd is undeterred. The angry chanting of, "We won't be moved!" can be heard over and over again like waves of determination. We're quite a distance from where the shots have been fired although we have a clear view of the whole area from where we are stood, on the hilltop between the National Theatre and the Intercontinental hotel.

Since some of the people in the crowd had turned up with young children, some even with babies, many among the crowd are now urging parents to take the children home. "The line of fire is no place for children," I hear it being said from different parts of the crowd, followed by, "We need the children to live, after all it is for them we are doing all of this." There is movement in the crowd as all around us families with children start leaving the area.

"We should go, too," says my friend. "You are a child, too, you know."

I half laugh and protest, "But I want to be part of this, we can't leave now!" Though she's not to be persuaded.

"I don't want to have to explain to your grandma why you're lying dead in University Square when you were only supposed to be at my house! We need to go. Now!"

I think of Mutti and how she must be out of her mind with worry by now, given how it's long past my curfew. Eventually, I give in and we slowly start walking away from the crowd, trying to find a way out of the square which is not blocked by the army. In the end we find an exit, a narrow side road and hurry towards home, leaving behind the crowd and the chanting of, "I'd rather be dead than be a communist!"

On our walk home, we are confronted by the sight of tens and tens of army vehicles approaching the area neighbouring the square and parking up. We see what looks like hundreds, if not thousands, of soldiers getting out and hurriedly marching towards the square we had just left behind. We keep our heads down and carry on walking. It becomes obvious that an arduous fight will no doubt ensue. For those brave people staying behind in the square it will be a long night. I say a little prayer for them, these incredibly determined people, willing to give their lives in the pursuit of a better life.

When I finally get home I try to think of an excuse for Mutti as to why I'm so late, for it's well past midnight. Never mind, I shouldn't have bothered. Mutti is still up, waiting for me. She greets me with, "I told you not to go out there! You never listen! Do you really want to get yourself killed? I've been watching out of the window, how one ambulance after another has been bringing wounded people to A&E. Out there, at the moment, there is no place to be, not for a child your age!" I tell her that I'm hardly a child, I am 16 years old after all, but there is no arguing with Mutti. "I'm so disappointed that you lied to me," she says and I feel really bad for I don't like upsetting or disappointing her.

She relents in the end, offers to make me a hot chocolate. Her anger has now subsided and as she makes my hot chocolate, she can't help to excitedly ask, "So, what's going on out there? What are the latest news?" I tell her about the crowd at University Square, their determination to see change through, the army opening fire and finally the mass of soldiers rushing out of their army vehicles and making their way towards the square we had already left behind. When I finally get into bed, I say a prayer of gratitude for having lived to experience this momentous day and also for those brave people facing the army in University Square before I drift off to sleep.

The following morning I wake up late. It's gone 9.30 am and I am annoyed with myself because I would have liked to wake up earlier and find out what course the previous night's events took, what are the latest developments. I have a quick breakfast with my sister. I'm thinking of calling Dani, getting dressed and going out with her for a little. Mutti is having a coffee next to me, in the kitchen, listening to the radio. We chat a little about this and that when all of a sudden the radio program is interrupted by the announcement that martial law is in place across the country. This is shortly followed by a communique by Ceausescu with the flash news that the minister for defence, had been sacked for being a traitor, and that he, the minister, thereafter committed suicide this morning. Both Mutti and I are speechless and look at each other puzzled. Why is the minister deemed a traitor, we ask ourselves, but no other details regarding the incident are relayed.

Straight after, I call my friend. She doesn't have any fresh news herself so we decide to go out to witness for ourselves what turn the protest took overnight. I plead with Mutti to let me go out, I tell her that I'm not going to venture far from the flat, just to the end of the road. I just want to hear what has been happening, get a feel of what's occurred overnight and what mood Bucharest is experiencing now. She allows me to go out but just for an hour or so. She reminds me that this afternoon all four of us are supposed to be getting a lift from one of her friends to mum's house, so that we can all spend a few days of Christmas together. I get dressed warmly, give my little sister a quick hug and kiss and run out to meet my friend, Dani, who is waiting for me in front of the building.

It's another beautiful, sunny but crisp winter's morning. Uncharacteristically dry and no snow for this time of the year. We start walking towards the main road, Calea Dorobantilor. All the roads leading to the main road are literally deserted. "What's going on? Is everyone sleeping late?"

As we approach the main road, it soon becomes obvious that everyone is where the action is. We hear the roar of the crowds even before we hit the main road which is packed full of people for as far as the eye can see. On the pavement, in the middle of the road and most amazingly atop army tanks, waving flags with the communist symbols cut out, shaking hands with and embracing the soldiers. Voices of, "We've won, we've won!" can be heard from every corner alongside of, "The army is on our side!" Both my friend and I feel elated at the news and the contagious atmosphere of sheer joy of realising that the people have come through vincible.

"Where is everyone going?" we eventually ask a group of people walking alongside us.

"The TV station headquarters. We're going to claim our freedom of speech."

My friend and I walk with the crowds, and she gets spotted by some friends who are atop a tank. They wave us over straight away. "C'mon, jump up!" they say to us and we don't need much encouragement to climb up, on top of the tank. It's only now, from this height, that we see the sheer volume of the crowd walking not just in front, but mostly behind us.

"Where are all this people coming from?" we ask.

"University Square, though some joined at Piata Romana," someone answers. "Last night, the army kept opening fire until the early morning, in University Square. So many people died, even more injured. In the end, at about 3 o'clock in the morning the crowd finally fled, couldn't take it anymore. It looked like a lost cause... But, come the morning the people started flocking back, again. Even bigger numbers than last night if you can image it! They literally poured into the square like a flood that burst the gates.

"Soon, it became obvious that the army was no longer able to control the flow. Nor willing to open fire again. We took it that they were finally on our side. We knew then that the fight at University Square had been won by the will of the people. After a while some people decided to walk to the CC palace where Ceausescu is supposed to be cooped up to force him to step down. And some of us decided to go to the TV headquarters so we can make our victory public to the whole country. That's where we're all headed now!"

We're slowly moving in that direction, past my school, which is closed for the holidays and past the bookshop opposite. Surprisingly, the bookshop is open and a bunch of people run in and come back out carrying armfuls of Ceausescu's books. They pile them all up in the middle of the road. Then, someone gets out a lighter and sets them all on fire. More people go inside the library and come out carrying even more books bearing Ceausescu's face on their covers, which they promptly throw on the bonfire. We move on, getting closer, the tall building of the TV station now in full view. Our group and the tank besides of which we are now walking is almost towards the forefront of this huge crowd.

As we approach the TV station, I immediately notice army soldiers running on the roof top of the building, then throwing themselves on their front, guns pointing at us. I must be one of the many to notice them as some other people, quite probably already terrified by the army's actions of the previous night, start screaming and running for cover, trying to find some refuge in the side roads. We quickly follow my friend's group of friends. We also take refuge on a side road but don't venture far. We still have a good view of the TV building in front of us.

We notice a small group who had broken off from the crowd, forcing their way inside the TV building. For a few moments nothing happens and we all – both protesters in the street and soldiers up, on the rooftop – wait in silent and tense anticipation for the next move. We have no idea what's happening inside – things could be going either way… So we wait. The small group eventually reappears on the rooftop. We all gasp in delight from down below as they start walking towards the snipers. By this point it's obvious that the snipers are unlikely to shoot, but we are all amazed and delighted to see that the group is greeted with an extended handshake by an officer. Following this gesture, the soldiers who had been pointing their guns at the crowds, abandon their position and they also make their way to the small group of protesters, one by one offering their outstretched hand to shake theirs. The crowd below claps frantically as a feeling of relief and euphoria takes over. Then one of the protesters on the rooftop hands something to the officer which together they open up fully. It's a long, homemade banner simply stating that General Milea – the defence minister who had been reported to have shot himself earlier in the day and had been labelled a traitor on the radio that morning – had in fact died a hero for refusing Ceausescu's orders to shoot civilians. It's a poignant moment and people in the crowd bow their heads for a moment, out of respect.

The spell of the moment, however, is broken by the sound of a helicopter now flying above the TV station building. Everyone assumes it must be the Ceausescus fleeing. People boo, shout "traitors", "criminals", "scum" until the helicopter is out of sight.

"Where do you think they are fleeing to, if it is indeed, them?" I hear someone asking.

"China, Russia?" someone from the crowd answers back.

"Maybe Iran, where he's just come back from that visit, the other day. In truth, there aren't many places left in the world willing to welcome them with open arms…"

The conversation is interrupted by a group of people who have appeared on the balcony of the TV building enthusiastically exclaiming, "Dear friends, we have won! We are now broadcasting live from the freed TV station."

This news is met by huge cheers. Some people recognise the personalities on the balcony and are explaining to those within earshot who is who. My friend, Dani and I look at each other gleefully and we excitedly decide that, since the TV station is broadcasting freely, we ought to go back home so we can see it for ourselves, to watch live the evolving events.

Back at Mutti's flat, we are greeted by a jubilant Mutti. The telly is already on and she and my great-grandmother are toasting the news with a glass of champagne. As soon as we walk through the door, we all hug and kiss each other elated at the turnaround of events.

"I went out and got a bottle of champagne," Mutti explains. "I couldn't resist! I know I normally wouldn't dream of it, but today you must have a small glass with us. We must celebrate. A miracle has just happened!" she exclaims.

"Oh, you can say that again!" my great-grandmother chimes in. "I've been waiting for this moment for almost half a century! The almighty has been gracious enough to allow me to witness this moment, to see the communists tossed out of power! We must certainly toast this miraculous moment!"

We all settle in the living room, and watch the TV, mesmerised. All sorts of different people come on air and recall the events of the previous night as well as this morning, which culminated in the Ceausescus fleeing in their helicopter and therefore in the accomplishment of the will of the people for, hopefully, a democratic future for the country.

However, not before long we have to leave the comfort of the sitting room sofa, as Mutti's friend has already arrived to give us a lift to mum's house. She urges us to leave immediately, because she is aware that most of the roads leading out of the city centre, where Mutti lives, are closed. She believes that she would have to take many detours to find alternative routes to get us to mum's. Besides we are also taking Mammy, my great-grandma, with us who is finding it increasingly difficult to walk. For her, the descent down the stairs and the walk to the car is extremely slow and painful. Once we are all in the car, Mutti's friend starts driving us to mum's house, half following her intuition and half guided by some of the road deviation signs, many of which are no longer relevant. Eventually and much later than expected, we get there…

Mum comes out to the car and helps us unload at the other end. Soon enough we are settled in front of the TV again, watching the latest developments. The live coverage of the events developing in Bucharest and the rest of the country is chaotic with many statements of the broadcast disputed or rejected later on in the day. However, during the remainder of the evening two events seem to be undisputed – firstly, that a new ad hoc temporary government is now in power and that a new wave of attacks on key buildings by unknown factions labelled as terrorists, loyal to the Ceausescus, is under way. Moreover, the people, most of whom had left the streets, probably in the belief that with the Ceausescus out of the way, the will of the people and democracy had surely won, are now urged to take to the streets once more to protect the fledgling democracy of the country. People choosing to stay at home are advised to close their curtains in order to avoid becoming a target for the terrorists.

Over the next couple of days the whole family is glued to the telly, watching reports of more and more deaths at the hands of these unknown terrorists, who is claimed, are willing to fight to their very last breath to defend the former regime and its leader. The centre of Bucharest looks, given the few images available on the telly, like a war zone – with tanks and army vehicles out in full force again, this time protecting the fledgling democracy as well as the key institutions of the city.

"Will this never end?" my mother says out loud. "Or will it all end in a civil war?" she asks, though, of course, there is no one to know that answer for sure.

My father also calls daily now and he himself is tense, eager to get updates about the latest situation inside the country – our family reunion is very much in the balance, everything hanging on the hope that the violence will soon subdue and a peaceful and long lasting democracy will prevail.

The news broadcast also gives vague reports of the fleeing Ceausescus, who we are informed, had been caught and arrested by the new authorities whilst apparently on their way to a 'safe house' in Targoviste, where it is claimed that Ceausescu intended to 'build a strategy' to overcome what he considered to be a coup d'état. Upon hearing the whereabouts of his arrest, I can see that my mum is startled. She turns to me to say,

"Wow! A safe house in Targoviste? I bet that would be Vergil's grandparents' house that they were heading for! The house where Ceausescu felt safe in his youth, when he helped Vergil's grandfather mobilise the communist strategy!" We both shrug our shoulders as, of course, who is to know for sure what exactly had gone through Ceausescu's head at that time and what his true motivation might have been in heading for Targoviste...

Christmas Day arrives and due to the events of the past few days provisions are low, as most shops had been closed for business and the few which remained open had barely any products to sell. Mutti however, pulls a few favours with friends and neighbours and manages to prepare a delicious meal for us. It's gone lunchtime and the TV news presenter continually asks the audience to stay tuned for important and imminent developments regarding the Ceausescus. In fact, this information is relayed so many times, that by the end of the afternoon, we all feel deflated since still nothing concrete appears to materialise.

Then, early evening, quite unexpectedly we are told that Ceausescu's trial is to follow next. We all sit down in front of the telly and start watching as the trial begins. Within seconds of the trial opening, upon hearing the introductory statements, my mum gasps.

"My good God, the judge! The judge! It's the same one as at your father's trial. I'd recognise that voice anywhere..."

No faces other than the Ceausescus are made visible on screen and the names of those officials making up the court are being kept secret. However, time will prove my mother correct, for in due time, the names of all those who took part in Ceausescu's trial are made public and the judge is proven to be indeed, Gica Popa, the very same who presided over my father's trial and passed his death sentence.

We watch, perhaps an hour or so of footage, as the Ceausescus, sitting side by side, in a secret military installation, are accused by the ad-hoc military tribunal of genocide, treason by undermining the state power and economy, and desertion by attempting to flee the country, among others. Except for the genocide part, the same charges as those which had been brought against my own father, only a few months before.

At most times, the trial seems like a macabre farcical comedy, with Ceausescu refusing to accept the legitimacy of the court, being bewildered by some of the accusations and displaying no understanding, no remorse nor empathy for the extent to which he abused the people he ruled over for so many decades. At one point, confusingly even to us, the spectators watching at home, even Ceausescu's own appointed solicitors no longer defend him and start to side with the prosecution, accusing him of said crimes.

My mum spends almost the entire duration of the trial open mouthed, shaking her head.

"What on earth is this? This is not the kind of trial expected of a democratic country. This is the same kind of a Stalinist-style show trial that your father and I went through with the verdict decided no doubt before the Tribunal had even been created! This says to me that nothing has changed politically – just some of the faces of those in power."

Finally, the Ceausescus' sentence is read out and the judge, Gica Popa, issues a concluding monologue.

"Word for word like the one delivered at your father's trial. He has obviously only ever learned by heart one closing statement!" my mother says, sarcastically.

Straight after his closing statement, the judge declares that the sentencing of death, executed by firing squad, will be effective immediately, at which even Ceausescu retorts, "We could have been shot without going through this masquerade!"

My mum is also baffled by the lack of legal and lawful compliance. "Effective immediately? That can't be legal even by communist standards! Even your father was granted due time to appeal his death sentence, if he wished to do so!" my mum continues, appalled at the proceedings. "The Ceausescus have ripped the heart out of this country and its people and I surely think they do deserve the capital punishment, but! But! I guess only time will perhaps tell if I'm the only one sat here in front of the TV, wishing to see justice done fairly and justly, complying with some kind of standards of law. Because otherwise, how could the new government be instilling any faith in a different or a democratic future, if this is the tone they are setting, with this kind of a trial?" my mother frowns, full of concern.

We watch on, in stunned silence, as the Ceausescus plead for their lives before being silenced once and for all, by a rain of bullets. Then darkness. Silence. The end.

The end of what, though, we are all left pondering.

The TV coverage continues from the TV studio, where presenters and their guests speculate that now, perhaps and finally, these rogue factions, loyal to the Ceausescus and which have terrorised much of the country over the past few days, will finally put their arms down, so that people could start going about their daily lives in peace and democracy would be allowed to flourish.

My mum and dad hope as much, too, as they start over the ensuing days to make plans for when that would happen. My father tells my mum that he had already purchased plane tickets for us, valid from as soon as the airport in Bucharest opens and commercial flights would resume again. But, of course, there is also the fact that we need not just plane tickets to get to him, but passports and visas for the UK, too, where it transpires that my father is residing. He assures us that regarding the visas, it would only be a matter of formality. We would need to go to the British consulate in Bucharest, he explains, make an appointment for the purpose of collecting our visas and then retrieve them once we had acquired the passports. *But, how?* My mum and I keep wondering, how are we going to get damn passports when the whole country and all of its institutions are still in lockdown and chaos rules?

Slowly and gradually, over the next few days, following the Ceausescus' deaths, the terrorist forces do indeed, start putting down their weapons. At the same time, in the first few days of the New Year, the new government gets to work and reopens various government institutions including the airport. Flights are to resume their schedules in a matter of days, the public is informed. And as luck would have it, we find out that one of my father's uncles is appointed the new head of the national police force. Jean Moldoveanu, had been the only one on my father's side of the family not to have condemned my father's decision to defect. He himself having had become vocally disillusioned with the communist regime and therefore side-lined by Ceausescu from his ministerial position in the late '70s, he understood better than many others my father's motivations in defecting and thus, trying to help his country from afar. Now, rehabilitated by the new administration, Jean is to head the national police force under the new government.

We find out about his new appointment incidentally, by watching the news one evening. As soon as my mother becomes aware of it, she gets in contact with him and asks him for help with the required procedure of getting passports for the three of us – my mum, my little sister and myself. He promises he would guide us through the process of application and true to his word, he does so. Within days, we are in possession of our passports.

Now, having already taken possession not only of the passports but of the plane tickets too, the next step is to get our visas. Again, my father assures us that we would get them as soon as we make an appointment at the British consulate to that effect.

And so, we make our way to the consulate, early one morning, where once we get there, we are faced with a never ending queue of people. People who are there for the same purpose – to get visas for the UK to visit families which they have been separated from, in certain situations for decades… We finally manage to get an appointment – after having queued up in the freezing cold for over six hours over two days. But, in the end, we manage to make the required appointment which is to be for the following day.

The following day arrives and both my mother and I turn up at the consulate house in time for our appointment. There are many other people there, in the waiting room with a similar time to ours, also for their appointments to get their visas. The procedure transpires to be that when your name is called, you approach one of the two windows which are manned by Romanian speaking assistants. The passports are handed over to the people behind the said window and after having the details checked over, the visa would be applied and the passports handed back.

Our name is finally called, but just before we reach the window, we notice one of the assistants behind it, walking round and asking us to follow her. We follow her out of this area, down a corridor then another one, into a small room.

"What's going on?" my mum asks puzzled.

"Please take a seat and wait to be called in," the person who had shown us the way, answers impartially, pointing at the row of chairs, without even glancing at us nor answering my mum's question.

"To be called in where?" asks my mum without taking up the offer of a seat.

"The consul wishes to speak to you regarding the visas," the woman simply retorts.

"OK," my mum says and I can tell by the tone of her voice that she's uncertain as to what to make of it.

We stand, waiting, without talking. After a short while, an older man appears. He looks my mum up and down and tells her in English, "This way, please."

He opens a door and ushers us in. My mum walks in, ahead of me, and as she walks through the door I can see her hesitating for the briefest of seconds. I walk in right behind her and look around the room. I realise straight away the reason for her hesitation. For the setup of the room into which we have been ushered has an uncanny resemblance to the interrogation room at Calea Rahovei, the very same room my mum and I had been interrogated in. Two desks almost perpendicular to each other with one of the desks having a window and a radiator behind it, whilst the other displaying a clock above it and a wireless on a shelf, behind one of the desks. Instead of the desk and chair at which I had sat in Calea Rahovei, in the interrogation room, in this room there is a small coffee table. Pretty much the same colour and size as that very desk where I had been asked to sign the dreaded incriminating declaration, which I refused to do. The only difference regarding the setup is that instead of a wooden chair behind the table there stand two upholstered chairs. On closer inspection there is no picture of Ceausescu hanging proudly either, but instead a picture of the Queen Elizabeth II is displayed on a wall.

The man who had ushered us in, quietly blends in the background of the room. And upon seeing us come in, a short woman maybe in her early forties, gets up from behind one of the desks and walks round.

"State your names, please," she says abruptly by way of greeting us. My mum raises an eyebrow in response but hears me giving her my name and she obliges to do so herself. I can tell she's far from pleased to be spoken to so in such a curt manner. The woman mumbles her own name which we don't really catch as she peers at some papers in her hand.

"Take a seat," she says waving at the chairs by the coffee table. I don't pay her much attention at first for I still can't take my eyes off the set up of the room, wondering if my brain is playing tricks on me. *Am I back in Calea Rahovei?* I keep asking myself. *I can't be. This is the British Embassy and Consulate, for sure. Snap out of it! After all, it is no more than an office and they all tend to look alike!* I tell myself again and again.

I perch on the arm of my mum's armchair and when I eventually turn my eyes upon the woman now sitting across from us, I see that her face is devoid of makeup and she is extremely pale. She has short, grey hair, styled in a Caesar cut and given the grey shirt and greyish-green skirt she is wearing, she comes across as a depressing entity of ash. I take it that she must be the Consul and the man standing in the shadows, blending in the background, her secretary, perhaps. Or is it, that he might be the Consul, watching from the shadows and she, his secretary? I can't be certain. I should have paid better attention when she mumbled her introduction to us. She's talking to us in English and because my mum's spoken English is not great, I start translating for both.

"What is the purpose of your visit to the UK?" the woman asks us. My mum asks me to tell her about going to see my dad who is residing in the UK.

"If you wish for the family to be together, why is he not the one coming over here, to Romania, to see you?" she now demands to know. My mum raises an eyebrow and stares at her incredulously and in silence for a moment. Then she asks me to explain to her that my father was a political defector, sentenced to death in absentia, and given the current political uncertainty of the country there are no guarantees that his life would not be in danger if he were to return over here.

"So, you intend for the family to be reunited, to stay for good in the UK?" she asks, looking, for no clear reason, suspiciously at my mum.

My mother hesitates before asking me to tell her, "If the circumstances will be right."

The woman does not reply straight away. She leans back in her chair, folding her arms studying us, firstly looking at me and then intently at my mother. It feels uncomfortable to be scrutinised so I fidget a little. I nervously look over at my mum, who, straight back and chin held high as ever, is quietly staring right back at this woman. Never one to be easily stared down, my mother. Eventually, the grey woman speaks again.

"You see, it is at the discretion of the consul general to whom visas are granted, pending on what merit is deserved. And so, given this particular situation, I will take the liberty to refuse granting your visas," she says as she waves in the air, the papers held in her hand, as she carries on, "in the assertion that your family does not qualify for the purpose of these visas. The understanding now is, that your intention might be to remain in the UK for good. And as such, I am not prepared to grant visas, the purpose of which might later on be misused."

I look over at mum and start translating but mum says not to bother as she has grasped perfect understanding of what was said. My mum gets up without saying a word nor waiting for anyone else to say anything further. She heads for the door and I follow suit straight away.

As we walk out of the door, we hear the woman saying behind us, "That's all. You may go now," though we are already well out of the door by now.

The man who had seen us in, quickly runs out after us, overtakes us and starts leading us towards the exit. I can tell that my mum is furious. She's not saying a word, but given her furious stomping, I can tell. We continue not to talk as we make our way out of the British Embassy and Consulate grounds, and onwards to home.

Once home, my mum paces up and down as she awaits my father's call. When he finally does call, my mum gives him the details of the day's events at the consulate. My father asks my mum not to get emotionally involved and to return to the consulate the following day. He promises that he would make certain that this time round, the visas will be granted without any further dramas or questions. Despite my mother's initial protests at this idea, we find ourselves back at the British consulate the following day. And this time, when we present ourselves at the glass window, our passports are taken from us, only to be returned with the visas stamped inside them, a few minutes later. Both my mum and I look at each other and allow to give out a loud sigh of relief.

The airport has now opened and is operational, with our flight confirmed for the following week. It is now that I start to contemplate for real the prospect of leaving behind the life that I had become accustomed to in order to start a new one. The thought leaves me somewhat melancholic for a while, but then my little sister walks into the room, comes to sit on my lap and puts her arms round my neck. And just like that, I know for sure that I never want to be separated from her, ever again, and so the melancholy all but disappears.

It's the day before our departure and I don't know whether I'm anxious or excited at the prospect of what the future might bring, but I had a restless night's sleep. I wake up early and go to the kitchen to make myself a hot drink. The light is on in the kitchen and when I open the door I see that my mum is up already, too, a cup of coffee in front of her.

"Couldn't sleep anymore either?" she asks with a smile.

"No," I reply as I look for a cup to make myself a hot chocolate. She watches me for a few seconds and I can tell that there's something she wants to tell me but doesn't quite know how to start. Eventually, she speaks.

"You know, with us leaving tomorrow, there is one place we both need to go to before we leave."

"Oh?" I say, unsure what she is talking about.

"We need to go back to Calea Rahovei, you know…" At hearing her say the name of that dreaded place, I clumsily drop my cup and spill hot chocolate everywhere.

"What would you want to go back there for?" I ask her, wondering if she had lost her mind.

"I think we both need to go," she continues calmly, frowning. "We never had a chance to say thank you to the guard who looked after you, back then, you know, when you were held there. And it's only right that we do so."

I look at her, incredulous, almost letting out a gasp, for until this moment I hadn't even realised that my mother knew the details of my ordeal back at Calea Rahovei.

At the time, following my return home, both Mutti and Mammy asked me straight away to give them a detailed account of what had happened. I had done so on condition for them not to ask me to speak about it thereafter, ever again. However, my mother had not once asked me any questions about what had occurred during those days I had been detained there. So, now, her being aware of knowing the details of my ordeal, shocks me almost as much as her insistence to go back to that forsaken place.

"Oh, don't look so surprised! I heard you telling Mutti and Mammy what happened back then. I never asked you about it because I never wanted you to relive that nightmare. Some things in life are better buried and forgotten… Still, it's only right we go and say our thanks to that man."

And so, we get dressed and call for a taxi to make the journey once again to Calea Rahovei. We both go downstairs and get into the taxi like we did all those months ago. Only that this time we are doing so willingly. My mum gives the taxi driver the address, "Calea Rahovei, number 36," just like she had done back then.

And just like the taxi driver had done back then, this guy also turns around in surprise and asks my mum, "What would you want to go there for, ma'am?"

Only that this time instead of being met by tearful eyes filled with petrifying fear and a frosty retort, both my mum and I smile at his obvious surprise. My mum explains that there is someone we need to go and see there.

"Oh, haven't you heard?" the driver replies straight away. "All the political prisoners have been released from there. The minute the Ceausescus fled. And I heard that the tyrants who ran that place have now fled for their lives. They're hiding in whichever rat-hole they can find. They're afraid they would be lynched by the people, if they haven't been lynched already!"

Both my mum and I listen silently, as images of the torturing brutes of Vasile Gheorghe and his team of tyrants flash before my eyes, like the memory of a horrendous horror film.

Unlike last time, however, on this occasion the taxi driver drops us off right before the front gate, by the entrance to the compound. "I don't even know if there is anyone at all left in this place or what you might find there," the taxi driver says cautiously, before offering to wait for us.

"We might be a little while," my mum tells him, but he says that he doesn't mind the wait.

We walk up to the gated entrance, which all those months ago had been guarded by armed soldiers but is now abandoned. We walk gingerly into the courtyard and towards the main building, not quite knowing what to expect. We are met by deadly silence. My mum and I, we both wonder if the whole place might not indeed be deserted. We agree that this place is creepy enough as it stands, let alone being completely abandoned. Like walking into an empty house of horrors.

We walk through the main door and start calling out, "Hello, hello?" Silence. We call out again, a bit louder. And this time, we hear rushed footsteps behind a closed door. A second later, the door opens and a few young soldiers walk out and gather around us. They all recognise both my mother and myself straight away and give us a warm and smiley greeting, as if we might be long lost acquaintances. I don't recognise any of them and I doubt if my mother does either but she greets them equally warmly. It transpires that they, being army soldiers, are the only ones guarding the establishment now, having been left in charge, following the revolution. They explain how the army is in charge of all of the country's government institutions, until, "Things will settle and there will hopefully be some more clarity as to which department should be in charge of what." It also transpires that those *Securitate* beasts who used to run the place and conduct the abusive interrogations have now indeed fled for cover just as the driver had mentioned.

"They've all disappeared, they're all probably in hiding for the time being, ma'am," one of the soldiers tells my mum. "They don't know which way the wind will blow, if you see what I mean. Until it will become more obvious if they will be hounded or not for their past actions, they'll be lying low, no doubt."

My mum listens and nods and I see that she's just about to open her mouth to say something but doesn't quite get a chance to do so, as one of the other soldiers chips in, "But ma'am, miss! Are you here to pick up your stuff?"

My mum looks up at him, blinks puzzled and asks, "What stuff would that be?"

The soldier then starts walking down the corridor as he beckons us. "Come! This way."

We follow him, intrigued, through a door, off the dark corridor.

"There's a huge cardboard box with your name on it, in here," the soldier carries on saying. "You can have it back now. Lots of other people who had their stuff taken away, have come back here, over the past few days, since the revolution, to collect their stuff. Isn't that why you're here?" he asks, now him being the one who is all of a sudden intrigued and puzzled, by our presence here.

My mum doesn't quite get a chance to explain why we are here, for we are already in the middle of a huge room, the floor of which is covered by tens and tens of boxes with different names and numbers written over them.

The soldier seemingly forgets what he had just asked us, and he starts walking in between the boxes, looking around and exclaiming, "Oh, where is your box? I saw it with my own eyes the other day, when someone else was looking for their own box…"

My mum and I also start looking around for it. We notice boxes full of VCRs and VCR tapes, Walkman Personal Stereos, stereo systems, old clocks, light fittings, paintings, old books, and the list can go on and on…

"Found it!" the soldier cries out victorious. "I knew it was here, somewhere!"

Both my mum and I rush to the box, eager to see what it contains inside. "Can it be…?" I ask myself and I'm sure that my mum is thinking the same thing, for when she reaches out to open the box I can see that her hands are slightly shaking, nervously.

My mum tears off the sellotape binding the two halves of the top lid together and opens the brown cardboard box. We both look inside at the same time, almost bumping heads. And, yes there it is! My mum's hold-all bag which must have been taken from my friend's house that grim, November day, which marked the beginning of the ordeal our family endured for the two years which followed. My mum hurriedly opens the zip and starts rummaging through the bag. I can't properly see inside the bag, but my mum obviously can and judging by the wide smile on her face, it's all good news.

"I can't believe this! It's all here!" she says with a look of disbelief and unexpected joy.

"Oh, that's good news, ma'am, because bigger items would have gone to a different storage place, sometimes at the municipal police station."

My mum shakes her head. "There was my husband's carpet that was taken, and the TV and VCR, too, but I don't think we will need them that much where we are going!"

My mum lifts the hold-all bag out of the cardboard box and as the bag is lifted out, my mum gives out another squeak of delight.

"The photos! Look, Diana! The photo albums!" I take a look and indeed, right there at the bottom of the box are the albums of our family photos. We quickly grab one of the albums out and leaf through some of the pages for a few moments. Then we take out the rest of them. And right after everything has come out of the cardboard box, I notice a white envelope sitting right there, on the bottom of the box. I pick it up and open it to look inside it.

My mum is still leafing through one of the photo albums so she doesn't notice me looking inside the envelope, straight away.

"What's that?" she asks when she finally notices. I hand her the envelope and she looks inside. "The absolute bastards!" she exclaims, astonished. "I had almost forgotten that they had taken this money, too!"

For there in the envelope was a thick wad of dollars, money which my parents had saved up and which my mother was supposed to fall back on, as a cushion, in the eventuality of my father's defection.

We finally gather all of our stuff and it's now time for us to start making a move home. One of the soldiers asks my mum to sign a form to acknowledge that she has taken back ownership of the formerly sequestered goods. And as she signs the form she tells the soldier,

"I almost forgot why we came here! There was a guard, an elderly man who worked guarding the cells when Diana was incarcerated here. We don't know his name. Maybe any one of you does?" she asks and looks at them.

The soldiers all look at each other but they seem reluctant to say anything on the subject. In the end one of the soldiers breaks the silence.

"Yes, we know him. But, ma'am, despite the job he did, he was not a bad man, you know. Did he hurt Miss Diana at all? Is that why you're looking for him?"

My mum now understands their hesitation in talking about him and shakes her head straight away.

"No, no! Quite on the contrary! We're looking for him because he was so kind to Diana. He looked after her when he guarded the cell she was put in. We just wanted to thank him…"

All of a sudden, the soldiers then start smiling, noticeably feeling relieved. "He is retired now, ma'am. He retired maybe a couple of months after we stopped seeing both you and Miss Diana being summoned here," he concludes and I can tell that my mum is disappointed to hear that he is not around.

But then one of the other soldiers says, "He normally comes in every month to collect his pension. I'm sure he'll probably start coming back again, once things will settle down."

Hearing this, my mum smiles. She gets out of her handbag the envelope which she had just put inside it, a few moments earlier. She opens it and takes out four notes and stuffs one in each of the soldiers' hands. Her gesture is met with protests but my mum wouldn't have it.

"This is not from me! It's from Diana, to say thank you for looking after her family's heritage and for allowing her to be reunited with it," my mum says pointing at the hold-all bag. "So, please, don't be rude now, you boys have a drink on her!"

They all smile shyly in my direction, slightly bowing heads in thanks and I smile back.

Then mum gets a pen out from her handbag, and asks, "What did you say the old guard's name was?" which she writes on the back of the envelope. Turning to face the soldiers she says, "Can I ask of you to please give this to the old guard, next time he comes here?"

They all agree to do so. There is another form to sign to this effect and then one of the soldiers goes to put the envelope together with the form in a safe, whilst the other ones start walking us out, each helping us carry the photo albums and the hold-all bag to the waiting taxi.

After everything gets loaded into the boot of the taxi, my mum turns to the soldiers, the forth one now also having returned and joined the other three. The soldiers are all stood shoulder to shoulder waiting to see us off. My mum looks at them all with a slight smile on her face and tells them, "I always thought that, unlike the beasts who ran this place, you were good boys caught up in a nasty situation. I never thought I'd say this, but thank you. To all of you."

She puts her hand out to shake their hands but instead they all stand to attention and give her a military salute. My mum looks at them speechless, taken aback for a second. Then, she offers them a smile with a gentle nod of the head, before getting into the waiting car. Onwards!

It's the night before our departure to London, though is all becoming a bit of a blur. We have a big meal with family and a few of mine and mum's friends. We laugh, we cry, we reminisce and eventually we say our goodbyes as our friends all start to leave one by one.

In the morning, we wake up early and have breakfast. Before we know it, there is a taxi downstairs, waiting for us. My heart is breaking at having to say goodbye to Mutti and Mammy.

"You won't turn into an indifferent English girl and forget all about us," says Mutti and I laugh it off, promising them that I will be back to see them in no time. If only, though, I knew back then that it would be another four years before I'd be able to see either of them again, I'm sure I would have hugged them a bit tighter and for a while longer. Nevertheless, the bond we all share, I know is there for eternity.

The taxi driver honks the horn and the three of us start rushing, grabbing bags, suitcases, waving goodbye, blowing kisses. At the airport, things happen in an equal blur and not before long we are sat in our seats, on the plane, looking out of the window as the plane takes off, leaving the city of Bucharest behind us.

Four hours or so later the plane lands in London, on a grey and rainy afternoon. Sad as I am at having had to say goodbye to Mutti and Mammy earlier, I am equally excited and a little nervous at the prospect of seeing my father for the first time in two years, two months and two weeks. I look over at my sister and I wonder if she would even remember much our father, for she was barely seven years old when we last saw him. But I shouldn't have worried, for the moment we step off the plane and my sister catches sight of our father, she runs up to him, arms outstretched to hug him.

We all take turns to hug him and him us, all of us shedding a tear of sadness at the time spent apart, a tear of joy at finally and thankfully being reunited, before collecting our luggage and walking together towards a new chapter of our lives.

The End